PETER ABRAHAMS was born in 1919 in Johannesburg, South Africa. His collection of short stories *Dark Testament* (1942) was followed by the publication of his first novel, *Mine Boy* (1946), which established Abrahams as an important novelist. He has since published eight works: *Song of the City* (1945), *Path of Thunder* (1948), *Wild Conquest* (1950), *A Wreath for Vdomo* (1956), *A Night of their Own* (1965), *This Island Now* (1966), the autobiographical *Tell Freedom; Memories of Africa* (1954), and an essay *Return to Goli* (1953).

He attended St Peter's College in South Africa in 1939 and then went to sea for two years as a stoker during the war before settling in Britain. There he joined the editorial staff of the communist newspaper, *The Daily Worker* and began to write in earnest.

Abrahams finally settled in Jamaica, in 1957 with his wife and family where he became editor of the *West Indian Economist*, a commentator on Jamaica's radio and television and a radio news network controller of *West Indian News*.

Heinemann Educational Publishers
A division of Heinemann Publishers (Oxford) Ltd
Halley Court, Jordan Hill, Oxford OX2 8EJ

Heinemann: A division of Reed Publishing (USA) Inc.
361 Hanover Street, Portsmouth, NH 03801-3912, USA

Heinemann Educational Books (Nigeria) Ltd
PMB 5205, Ibadan
Heinemann Educational Boleswa
PO Box 10103, Village Post Office, Gaborone, Botswana

FLORENCE   PRAGUE   PARIS   MADRID
ATHENS   MELBOURNE   JOHANNESBURG
AUCKLAND   SINGAPORE   TOKYO
CHICAGO   SAO PAULO

First published by Faber & Faber Ltd 1946
First published in the *African Writers Series* 1963
Reprinted (six times)
Reset 1975
Reprinted (eight times)
First published in this edition 1989

ISBN 0 435 90562 7

Printed and bound in Great Britain by
Cox & Wyman Ltd, Reading, Berkshire

94 95 96 12 11 10 9 8 7

PETER ABRAHAMS

MINE BOY

Illustrated by Ruth Yudelowitz

HEINEMANN

This book is for 'Dusty'

*But there is neither East nor West, Border, nor
Breed nor Birth,
When two strong men stand face to face,
Though they come from the ends of the earth!*
                                        KIPLING

ONE

Somewhere in the distance a clock chimed. The big man listened.
One . . . Two . . . Three. . . . Three o'clock in the morning.

He shifted the little bundle from his right hand to his left,
hitched up his pants, and continued up the narrow street. A dark
narrow street full of shadows, he thought. But then this whole
Malay Camp is full of shadows.

I wonder where I am, he thought. He had lost all sense of direction. Still, one street was as good as another. . . .

And then he saw the woman at the gate. He would have passed
without seeing her, for she was a part of the shadowy gate, but she
had coughed and moved. He went closer.

'Sister, do you know a place where a man can rest and maybe
have a drink?' His voice was deep and husky.

'It is late,' the woman replied.

'It is very late,' the man said.

'Make a light for me to see you,' the woman said.

'I have no matches.'

'What have you?'

'Nothing.'

'And you want to rest and drink when it is so late?'

The man inclined his head, but the woman could not see it in the
dark.

'Have you money?'

'No.'

'Huh. You're a queer one. What are you called? Are you new
here?'

'Xuma. I come from the north.'

'Well, Xuma from the north, stay here and I will be back with a

1

light. Maybe you can have a rest and drink and maybe you cannot. But stay here.'

He saw the shadow move but heard no sound. He peered into the darkness of the gate. There was nothing but a wall of blackness to see. He shifted the little bundle from his left hand to his right and waited.

His legs ached with tiredness. There was a throbbing in his head that flowed from the emptiness of his stomach. His tongue felt thick with want of a smoke and drink.

Maybe, he thought – but would not allow his thoughts to go any further. Only a fool would break a door when someone had agreed to open it.

'Well, Xuma from the north, I am going to put the light on you. I warn you for your eyes. It is sharp.'

She had returned without him noticing. Like a shadow, he thought, and smiled to himself. And she has the voice of a strong person, he told himself.

'Put on the light,' he said.

The beam of a powerful torch struck his waist and lingered there for a moment, then swept down to his feet. From his feet it moved up inch by inch taking in the whole picture of him.

It started with the big, old tennis shoes that were kept together by bits of string and wire, and saw the toes peeping out in spite of the string and wire; moved up the dusty, colourless old trousers that were ripped at both knees and looked as though they would burst at the waist because they were so tight; up the immense chest and huge shoulders against which the equally tight and tattered shirt seemed to cling fearfully; it lingered on the broad, good-natured face for a brief moment; then it shifted to the right hand with its bundle and then the empty left hand. Then the torch snapped out and Xuma waited in the darkness.

'All right,' the woman said finally. 'You can have your rest and drink, Xuma from the north. Come.'

Xuma paused in the dark. The woman laughed in a deep rich voice.

'So big and strong and you are afraid!'

'It is dark, woman.'

Again the beam of light sprang into being, but this time it remained on the ground a few yards away from him.

'Come,' the woman repeated.

Xuma followed the beam of light.

'Here,' the woman said and pushed open a door. 'Come in.' Xuma followed her into the room. She shut the door and led the way to another room. This had a light and three men and an old woman sat at a table with a huge can of beer in front of them.

'This is Xuma from the north,' the woman said. 'He is tired and hungry. Give him food, Ma Plank. . . . Sit down, Xuma.'

Xuma looked at the woman. She was tall and big, with that smooth yellowness of the Basuto women, and she had sharp dark eyes. A strong woman, he decided, and those eyes can see right through a man.

'What do they call you?' he asked.

The woman smiled and he noticed that only one side of her face moved. The left side.

'Leah,' the woman said.

'What is it to you what she is called?' one of the men demanded. Xuma looked at the man. He was tall and thin and the youngest in the room. His mouth was twisted viciously and he glared at Xuma.

'Who is he?' Xuma asked the woman.

'That one is Dladla. He thinks he is a strong man and he plays with a knife, but he's a puppy.'

'Ho! And the mistress took the puppy to bed!' the eldest man at the table said and burst out in a cackling laugh.

Leah smiled. 'Yes, Daddy, why shouldn't the puppy please the mistress!'

Daddy's cackle increased. His sides shook. Tears streamed down his cheeks and he gasped for breath.

Dladla struck out suddenly. His fist caught Daddy on the side of the head and sent him flying into a corner. Xuma stepped forward and saw the knife in Dladla's hand.

Carefully Xuma placed his bundle on the table and circled round the long bench. Dladla raised the knife and showed his teeth. Each watched the other. A hush fell on the room. Daddy forgot that the side of his head hurt and gaped with open mouth and dancing eyes at this sudden prospect of a fight.

Ma Plank, coming into the room with the food Leah had

ordered her to get for Xuma, opened her mouth, shut it again, and went back to the kitchen.

'Give me that knife!' Leah commanded.

Dladla looked at her, then at Xuma, then back at her.

'No,' he said but there was a plea in his voice.

'Give!' Leah said, and this time her voice was hard. Dladla lowered his eyes and gave her the knife.

'Sit down! Both of you.'

'Women!' said Daddy bitterly from his corner and spat. 'They always spoil a good fight.'

'Ma Plank! Bring the food,' Leah called.

'Is the fight over?' Ma Plank asked without showing her face.

'There's another,' Daddy said and spat again. Then he leaned back against the wall and went to sleep.

'Eat,' Leah said when the old woman had put the food in front of Xuma.

Xuma looked at her and began to eat.

'You have fixed the holes properly?' Leah asked, looking at each of the others in turn.

In turn they nodded. She looked at Daddy's open mouth and smiled from the side of her face. 'And his?'

Ma Plank nodded.

'Then you can go to sleep,' Leah said.

Dladla and Ma Plank went out. Only the man who had been silent throughout remained. He looked at Leah then at Xuma.

'What is it?' Leah asked him.

'How do we know he's not from the police?' the man asked.

'I know,' Leah replied and her whole face creased in a smile.

The man nodded, then suddenly he held out his hand to Xuma. Xuma shook it. The man went out.

'Who is he?' Xuma asked.

'He is the brother of my man,' Leah replied.

'Your man?'

'Yes.' Her eyes softened. A half smile played round her lips. And as Xuma watched her it seemed that her face had grown weaker. Not so strong any more. And her eyes were not so sharp. They were just the eyes of a woman.

'Yes,' she repeated softly. 'My man. He's in jail. He's been there for one year, and he must stay there for another two years. He

4

killed a man. A big man with a big mouth who tried to kiss me. He is strong, my man, and he fights for his woman, and he kills for his woman. Not like Dladla who is all mouth and knife and nothing. He's a man, my man. You are a man yourself, Xuma, you are strong. But my man can break you like a stick! I don't lie, you can ask people. . . .'

She stopped speaking. The softness faded from her face and the old hardness returned. She looked at Xuma and smiled out of the side of her face.

From the corner came the sound of Daddy's snoring.

'And Dladla, what is he to you?'

She laughed a deep-throated laugh. 'A woman gets lonely for a plaything, that's all. . . . Now you, Xuma, what are you going to do?'

'I came for work. There is no work where I come from. And here, they say, there is much work.'

'Where will you work?'

'In the mines. It is a man's work.'

Leah shook her head and poured herself a drink.

'The mines are no good, Xuma, later on you cough and then you spit blood and you become weak and die. I have seen it many times. Today you are young and you are strong, and tomorrow you are thin and ready to die.'

'All work is like that.'

'No. . . . Listen Xuma, I like you, I can make you powerful. I am powerful here. If you become my head-man you will be powerful too. When you came and found me outside I was watching for the police. These others were burying beer in the ground. There is much money in it. Maybe you can work for me, heh?'

For a long while they looked at each other, then Leah smiled her full smile and shook her head.

'No. . . . Well, you are a man with the dumbness of a man. . . . Come, I will show you where you can sleep.'

'I have no money,' Xuma said.

'No. But you are strong and you will work and pay me later, heh?'

'Yes.'

'And maybe I will need a strong man sometimes and you will help.'

5

'Maybe.'

'Here,' Leah said, going into a little room, 'this is where the teacher lives but she will not come till day after tomorrow so you can sleep here. When she comes we will think of something else.' She struck a match and lit the candle. She went to the door. 'And listen to me Xuma from the north, don't think because I do this I am soft or easy and you can cheat me, because if you do, I will cut you up so that your own mother will not want you. . . .'

Xuma laughed. 'You are a strange woman. I don't understand you. The only thing I can understand is your kindness.'

'You're all right,' she said softly. 'But the city is a strange place. Good night.'

She went out and shut the door.

Slowly Xuma undressed. He felt better now that he had eaten, but he was very tired. Yet he found it hard to sleep when he got into bed.

A strange group of people, these, he thought. Nothing tied them down. They seem to believe in nothing. But well, they had given him a bed. She had given it to him. She who was the strangest of them all. And in the other room the old one they call Daddy was sleeping against a wall with an open mouth and with nothing to cover him. But life is strange. Yes, and these people are life. . . . Of course. . . .

TWO

The sun was high when Xuma woke. He lay still for a while and listened. But there was no sound from anywhere in the house.

'I must get up,' he sighed, and nestled back among the blankets. And then he remembered he was in the house of strangers and pushed back the blankets. They must not come in now, he thought, as he stood with only his shirt on. Quickly he dressed. There was not much to do. Only to slip on his pants.

He opened the door and stood listening. Somewhere in the house an alarm clock ticked. Tick. Tock. Tick. Tock. ... But that was all.

'Good morning!' he called.

No one responded.

'Good morning!' he yelled a little louder.

Still there was only silence.

'Hi!' he shouted.

A bee buzzed in through the door and circled over his head. He waved it away but it would not go. It buzzed closer. This fool thing will sting me, he decided, and hurried out of the room shutting the bee in.

The house was empty. He went through the kitchen into the yard. Then he heard voices. They came from the street. He went to the gate and looked out.

A crowd of people formed a ring in the street. And in the centre of the ring was old Daddy hopping around and shouting at the top of his voice.

Daddy's arms were flying and he jumped from one leg to the other dancing an old war dance and yelling ancient battle cries. Xuma smiled and pushed his way into the crowd.

On the ground were two coloured women. They were locked in battle. And the crowd was making bets as to who would win. Most of them favoured the thin dark woman who looked like an Indian. Lena they called her. The fat pale one they called Drunk Liz and didn't seem to like.

The fat one was on top, sitting on the chest of the little one. But the little one had her by the hair and was pulling. And tears were flowing from the fat one's eyes and her neck was pulled backward by the straining tug at her long brown hair.

'Pull! Pull them out, Lena!' Daddy shouted, and rolled into the gutter with excitement.

The little one pulled. The fat one loosened her grip on the little one's throat and fell back. As she tumbled over her dress went up and her pale flesh showed.

Xuma turned his eyes away.

The crowd roared. Daddy lay cackling in the gutter and kicking his feet in the air. Tears streamed from his eyes.

When Xuma looked again the little one was on top. And her left hand was on the throat of the fat one and her right hand was behind her back, searching for her shoe. She found it, raised it right above her head, and brought it down on the fat one's head.

When she lifted it again blood was flowing from the fat one's head. Xuma cursed under his breath. Daddy could not contain himself and rubbed his head against the pavement. Again the crowd roared. Xuma pushed his way through the crowd. He wanted to get away from it. He felt a strange heaviness on his heart.

'Stop it!' The voice carried above the roar of the crowd. Xuma turned and looked. It was Leah. The crowd made a passage for her. Without looking left or right she walked through till she stood over the fighting women. Her eyes blazed. Her arms were bare. She reached down and picked the thin woman up as though she were a child and flung her away from the fat one.

A few people in the crowd grumbled.

Leah flung back her head and smiled from the side of her face. Scorn burned in her eyes as they travelled over the crowd.

'I hear voices,' she said softly. 'Let me hear them again. I want to know them.'

She waited. No one spoke.

'Ah, so they are silent. That is good. But if anyone, man or woman, wants to fight or see a fight in front of my house, I am here.' She beat her chest with her fist. 'Come and fight me.'

In silence the crowd broke up and drifted away. Daddy got up and tottered drunkenly on his feet. The pale fat woman sat holding her bleeding head. She was sobbing. A little distance away the thin one leaned against a wall.

'Look! She's getting the horrors,' Daddy cackled gleefully, pointing at the thin woman.

Her mouth had slowly opened and a stream of saliva was trickling down on to her dress. Her body trembled. Her hands knotted into tight fists. Slowly she slid down the side of the wall till she lay stretched on the pavement. Her eyes glazed, and, but for the trembling of her body, she lay like one dead.

Leah spat in disgust, picked up the thin woman with the horrors and carried her into the yard.

Xuma and Daddy followed her.

'Bring me a sack,' Leah said.

Daddy brought the sack and spread it in the shade. Leah placed the woman on the sack and went to the gate of the yard.

'What are you sitting there for,' she called gruffly, 'come in here and wash the blood off that stupid head of yours.'

The pale, fat woman came in and washed her head under the tap. Leah filled a mug with cold water and went over and dashed it into the face of the woman with the horrors. The woman shivered convulsively, closed her mouth and the trembling grew less.

'Is she very sick?' Xuma asked, looking at the woman with the horrors.

Leah shook her head and pulled a mouth. 'Only one day she will get like that and she will not wake up any more. She's a good one that one, she's like Daddy. She knows life and she wants to forget it. . . . But you, how are you now? Have you had food?'

'I've been sleeping and when I got up there was no one in the house so I came out and I saw this fighting. Tell me, Daddy, is he always like this? He likes fighting, does he fight?'

'We will eat first and then we will talk and maybe later Joseph will take you to see the place, heh?'

Xuma followed her into the house and sat watching while she prepared the food.

9

For all her bigness she moved easily and gracefully. A tall strong woman with firm heavy hips. And it seemed to Xuma that again she was just an ordinary woman as she leaned over the fire to see that the meat did not burn. Like last night when she talked about her man who was in jail for having killed a man with a big mouth who had tried to make love to her. She was hard to understand, this woman. He shook his head.

She looked up.

'What is it?'

'Nothing.'

'Why do you shake your head? You look at me and then you shake your head. ... You think, she is strange this woman, she is hard and people fear her and for me she cooks, heh?'

'Yes.'

She laughed and there was something warm in her laughter. 'And you think, maybe she likes me, heh?'

'Yes.'

'Well, maybe I like, yes, but maybe you don't understand how. Maybe you think I like you to go to bed, heh?'

Xuma smiled but said nothing.

'Yes. ... I can see. But listen to me Xuma from the north, you are a baby with people. I can be your mother with people. Now listen to me, maybe you will understand and maybe you will not, but listen. I like you because you are here but you are not here. ... No. You don't understand. ... I am here, you see, I come from my people, but I am no longer of my people. It is so in the city and I have been here many years. And the city makes you strange to the ways of your people, you see?'

'Yes, yes. I see.'

'Good. ... Now eat.'

She pushed a plate of food in front of him and dished up another for herself. She sat facing him.

'You are from my people. ...'

'No, your people must be from the south.'

'You don't understand. Listen to me, you are from the north and I am from the south but the people are the same, heh?'

Xuma nodded doubtfully.

'You are a child. But listen, your people and my people have the tribal law and tribal custom, right?'

10

'Yes.'

'You come from there and you have the ways of our law, so I like you, but it doesn't mean I want to go to bed with you, oh no! And there'll be trouble if you misunderstand! I cannot make you understand, it's no use shaking your head. I know you don't understand. But maybe you will sometime!'

They finished eating and Leah took the plates and washed and dried them. She saw Daddy in the yard and called him.

'Daddy! Come in here.'

Daddy scowled and spat. 'What is it, woman. Can a man not be in peace for a minute.'

'Come in here, Daddy.'

He came, rolling drunkenly on his feet.

'Tell Xuma about the custom and the city.'

'Heh?' He rocked from side to side.

'Tell him about the custom and the city,' she repeated patiently, helping him into a chair.

'The custom and the city,' he murmured, then his eyes lighted up and he smiled. 'The custom and the city, ah. Oh yes, funny about the custom and city, Xuma. Very funny. Just you listen. . . .'

He got up and walked up and down the room. He rubbed his hands, smiled knowingly and smacked his lips. He lifted first one shoulder then the other.

'Very funny,' he said. 'One day the city came to visit the custom, Xuma. And the custom was kind. It gave the city food and it gave the city beer and it gave the city beautiful young women. . . .'

'No, Daddy,' Leah interrupted.

'Quiet, woman!' Daddy said very firmly.

Leah smiled.

'. . . As I was saying, it gave the city beautiful young women. And then what do you think? Unbelievable. The city didn't say a word. It didn't say "No thank you" and it didn't say "thank you". And the people said, "Ah, everything will be all right now, the custom and the city are friends." Hmmmm. . . . They did say that and they went out into the fields to look after their crops. And when the sun was going down they came back and looked for their beer but their beer was gone. And then they looked for the custom but he had gone too. And the city was there laughing at them. And now they go to jail if they drink beer. That's why I like beer. . . .'

Very funny, heh, Xuma? Well, that is it and I want to go to sleep. ...'

Daddy stumbled out. He circled the spot where the thin coloured woman who had been joined by the pale fat one, was sleeping off the effects of her horrors.

The two women who had fought each other lay side by side on the piece of sacking.

'There's no place here,' Daddy called out.

Leah went out with another sack and spread it for him a little distance away from the two women. Daddy stretched himself on his back and smiled up at her.

'I like you, Leah,' he said thickly.

'I like you, Daddy,' she replied.

'Then kiss me,' he demanded aggressively.

Leah knelt and kissed his forehead. When she got up he was fast asleep. A smile flitted across her face and disappeared. She stood looking at Daddy for a little while then turned and went into the house.

'You like him,' Xuma said.

'What is it to you,' she retorted, and there was a note of anger in her voice.

Xuma looked at her in silence. She brushed past him and went into another room. Xuma listened to her moving about. Picking up things and putting things away.

She began to hum. He recognized the song. It was the 'Rain Song'. Then she sang the words.

> *Mother it's raining*
> *And I'm getting wet*
> *It's cold and lonely*
> *And I'm getting wet*
> *Sad and lonely*
> *And I'm getting wet*
> *Mother it's raining*
> *And I'm getting*
> > *Getting wet.*

There was haunting sadness in her voice.

Xuma went into the yard and watched the three sleeping people.

From the house her voice drifted to him. But this time it was a gay song. Full of laughter and happiness and there was laughter in her voice as she sang it. It was a song of a conceited and boastful young man who went among the girls and told what a great and wonderful person he was, and who thought he was very handsome, so the girls set a trap for him one night and he ran five miles. And after that the girls mocked him day after day.

It was a song with many verses and they all had laughter and mockery for the boastful young man in them.

Xuma smiled and nodded. It served the young man right. The boastful one.

Then her singing stopped.

'Xuma!' her voice called.

He went back. 'Yes?'

Joseph, the brother of Leah's man, was there. Xuma looked at Leah. She smiled at him. There was no anger in her eyes.

'Joseph will take you to see the place. It is Saturday and there will be many customers and also the police, maybe, so we will be busy. Here is money. You can eat somewhere and come back later on, heh?'

'Who will help with selling?' Joseph asked.

'Those two sleeping and Daddy and Ma Plank, and I got two others coming. It is good that you go, Joseph. If they get you again there will be no fine.' She smiled at Joseph.

He nodded and led the way out. Xuma followed.

'Take care,' Leah called as they went down the street.

Joseph laughed and waved back. 'She's a good one,' he said to Xuma.

Xuma nodded and watched the crowded street.

'It is always like this on Saturdays. People have money in their pockets and it makes them move in the streets and they spend the money. Saturday is so here,' Joseph said.

It was so in all the streets. One street was as crowded as another. Groups of men and women milled up and down. It was Saturday. A national half holiday for the black citizens of Johannesburg. And Malay Camp shared with Vrededorp the honour of being the main social centres.

And the men in the streets spoke in loud voices and took out their purses and counted their money for others to see. And they wore their best and most colourful clothes. Red shirts and green shirts and yellow shirts and pink shirts. And they wore wide-bottomed trousers that swept the ground and tight jackets that reached down only as far as their waists. And sharp-pointed shoes.

And others wore only singlets and a pair of trousers to show how manly they were. And they were manly, these, they were tall and strong and their chests stood out and there were confident smiles in their eyes and they did not step aside but made others step aside.

Only if one big man in singlets meet another big man in singlets did they step aside. And then they would watch each other like sparring dogs, ready to jump.

They were called the strong men in Vrededorp and Malay Camp, and sometimes they would fight among themselves to determine the strongest. Two men would fight and the winner would fight another and another and another. And so it would go on till only two were left. And that would be the big fight. And the winner of that fight would be the strongest of the strong men.

Many men have died in these fights, for they fight with sticks and knives and shoes. Even stones.

And so on Saturdays they go up and down the streets of Malay Camp and Vrededorp with their chests out and an arrogant light in their eyes.

And on Saturdays too, the young women from The Hill and Berea and Park Town would be in Malay Camp. They would be dressed in the ways of white folk, only more colourfully, for they like brighter colours. And they would forget that they work on the Hill and in Berea and Park Town, and meet on street corners and talk at the top of their voices. And there would be much laughter and fun-making. And all of them would watch the men and talk about the men. And this one would say, I like that one. And another would say, I like that other there. And it would go on and they would point out the men they liked. Not with their fingers. With their eyes.

And in a mysterious way the men would know who each girl likes.

And after much dancing and laughter and showing of their legs by the girls, there would be a man and a girl and a man and a girl. And with more laughter and more loud talking a man and a girl would go away. They would go to drink in one of the many places. Or they would just walk. Or they would go to the Bioscope. Or they would go looking for a Maraba. Or they would just go. . . . And others would appear. And the same thing would happen.

And life would move slowly and excitingly. With much laughter and much shouting and talking and much drinking and much fighting. And the people of Malay Camp would stand on their verandahs and watch it all. And they would make remarks and go into the house and come out again and make more remarks.

And when night comes it would be even more exciting. . . .

'Saturday here is so,' Joseph repeated and offered Xuma a cigarette.

They stopped on a corner and watched the milling crowd. Across the way was the Bioscope and people were streaming in. Outside the Bioscope a little ring of men were playing dice. The man who had the dice executed an intricate dance before he flung the dice down.

A little further up the road two coloured men fought. They were like two punch-drunk boxers. They had been fighting for over an hour, and both only just managed to stay on their feet.

Still further up the road two 'swankies' were on their way down the road. They were dressed in violent purple suits with wide-bottomed trousers and long jackets that reached down to their knees, straw hats, red shirts and black ties. And each had a red handkerchief in the left hand and a light cane in the right. And they strutted and danced from the one side of the road to the other. They were both small and looked alike and the twin sets of clothes made them look like the same man twice.

A crowd of cheering and laughing people followed them.

A coloured man and a very pale woman passed Xuma and Joseph.

'Look at those black fools,' the woman said.

The man laughed.

Xuma felt a pang of shame and turned to Joseph.

'They are the fashion makers,' Joseph said.

'But it is foolish.'

Joseph looked at him and said nothing.

Suddenly a pick-up van swerved round a corner. Policemen jumped out and ran down the street. The crowd scattered.

15

'Come!' Joseph said.

People ran in all directions. The gamblers made a grab for the stakes and ran. The two 'swankies' disappeared down the street. Only the coloured people did not run.

'Come!' Joseph urged again.

'But we have done nothing.'

'They will not ask you,' Joseph said in disgust and dashed down the street.

A policeman was only ten yards away and he was coming straight at Xuma. Xuma waited. He had done nothing. He had just stood there watching. The policeman came nearer. He raised his stick and brought it down with force. It missed Xuma's head and struck his left shoulder. Pain shot through his body.

'I have done nothing,' he said and grabbed the policeman's arm before he could hit again.

'Let go! Bastard!' the policeman shouted and kicked out.

Xuma felt pain shooting up his leg.

'Dog!' he whispered and struck the policeman in the face. A look of strange surprise crept into the policeman's eyes. Xuma trembled with anger. He bunched his great fist and struck again. Hard. The policeman groaned and collapsed in a heap and lay still.

Xuma looked around. The van was still a distance away but two policemen were closing in on him.

'Now I will run,' he said and ran down the street.

'Stop that man,' one of the police shouted.

A coloured man stepped into the road and held up his hands. Xuma braced himself. His heart was pounding but he ran easily. He must be careful or this yellow bastard would deliver him to the police.

Another coloured man stepped into the road. Xuma felt afraid. To run and knock down two men at the same time was impossible. They would catch him. He could hear the feet of the policemen behind him. He hated the coloureds. He would hurt one of them before they got him. These half-castes!

An unbelievable thing happened. The second coloured man knocked the first one down and ran down the street waving to Xuma.

Xuma smiled and increased his pace.

'Thank you, brown man,' Xuma said.

'This way,' the man said and swerved into a passage, 'we will lose them.'

Xuma followed him.

They ran into a house and went through a window and over a wall. And into another house and over another wall. And the coloured people did not seem to mind. Then they walked down a narrow street and slipped into a house.

The coloured man locked the door then flopped down into a chair breathing heavily. He waved Xuma to a chair. Then he jumped up and looked out of the window.

The man's woman came into the room. She was black, Xuma noted with surprise. The man told her what had happened. Without a word she went out. She came back later with tea.

Xuma looked at the man. He was small and thin and there were many lines on his face though he was not old. And his eyes were red and he kept coughing. A dry hard cough that destroyed the lungs.

'Why did you strike the policeman?' the woman asked.

'The policeman struck him for no reason,' the coloured man said.

The woman looked searchingly at Xuma.

'It is so,' Xuma said.

The woman nodded. 'This one is a fool to meddle in other people's business.' She looked hard at her husband. 'His chest is bad. . . .' And then she smiled and her face looked very young and the tired lines disappeared and the eyes lost their sadness. 'But he is a good fool . . . Are you new to the city?'

Xuma nodded.

'That is why he struck the policeman,' the woman said to her husband.

The man took the woman's hand and smiled into her face.

'I must go,' Xuma said.

'It is not safe yet,' the man said. 'They will be looking for you still. Wait a little longer.'

THREE

Xuma had found the street without trouble. But it was difficult to find the house. The houses all looked the same in the gathering twilight. The same verandahs. The same yard gates. The same corrugated iron walls leaning drunkenly backwards. And all the same dirty colour.

And everywhere were people. People going into gates and coming out of gates. People staggering and falling. People fighting and cursing.

They had money and they wanted to get rid of it, Joseph had said. Saturday here is so, he had said.

'I say,' Xuma said to a passing stranger.

'Go to hell,' the stranger replied and kept going.

Xuma tried again. No one would stop and listen to him.

Then he saw the fat pale one who had been in the fight this morning, the one who had her head cracked. She was leaning against a tall drunk man. He went to her and touched her shoulder.

'Where is Leah's place?'

Drunk Liz looked at him with bleary eyes and shook her head.

'Go 'way, go 'way. I don't love you. This one's my daddy.'

'Go on,' the tall drunk man said and struck at Xuma.

Xuma dodged his blow and walked away. It is one of these gates, he thought, but which one? That pale one is stupid with drink. He stumbled into a person and grabbed him to avoid falling.

'Help! Help! They are robbing me!' Daddy cried, fighting desperately to get away.

'Shut up!' Xuma shook Daddy.

'Oh, it's you,' Daddy said. 'I thought you were in jail. Joseph said you would not run. Did you run?'

18

'Yes. Where is Leah's place?'

'I don't know,' Daddy said and walked away.

Xuma grabbed him and shook him.

'Come on, tell me!'

'Ho! So he thinks he's a lion because he knocked a policeman down, heh? Well, I'll show . . . Come on, fight!'

Daddy jumped away and walked round Xuma waving his fists. Then quickly he darted in and tapped Xuma's chest. Xuma laughed and grabbed at him. Daddy stepped back, slipped and fell. His head struck the pavement. Daddy groaned and lay still.

Xuma knelt and lifted his head.

'Are you all right, Daddy?'

Daddy grabbed Xuma's head and tried to pull him down.

'You old fox,' Xuma laughed.

He got up, carrying Daddy like a child in his arms. Daddy fought and struggled. But it was useless.

'Where is the place?'

'Well,' said Daddy slyly, 'I tell you what, will you buy me a drink if I take you there? That stupid Leah won't give me any more. Will you? If you say no I'll fight you and make a noise and I'll tell people you've robbed me and there will be trouble. . . .'

'All right,' Xuma said.

'You promise?'

'Yes.'

'May a million ants bite you if you lie?'

'Yes.'

'And may you get the horrors for a week. . . .'

'Go on! Show me the place.'

'I like you, Xuma.'

Xuma laughed.

'You'll get your drink, Daddy.'

'That's why I like you,' Daddy flung over his shoulder as he led the way.

There were people everywhere. People trying to get into the house for their drinks. Others trying to get out. And the whole place reeked of kaffir-beer.

Old Ma Plank sat over a huge vat in the yard and doled out scales of beer and collected shillings in return.

In the kitchen Joseph was busy doing the same thing.

'Xuma!' Joseph shouted. 'Xuma!'

He stopped his business and grabbed Xuma's hand and shook it vigorously.

'I thought they had taken you. I looked round once and saw you striking the policeman and I thought, now he's finished. Tell me, man, what happened?'

Xuma tried to tell Joseph but the noise was too great. He shook his head. Joseph nodded, slapped Xuma heartily on the back and offered him a scale of beer. Xuma shook his head. Daddy nudged him violently. He smiled and took the scale. Daddy beamed and patted his arm.

Xuma put the scale to his lips then passed it to Daddy. Daddy wiped his mouth with the back of his hand then raised the scale.

Just then Leah entered. She reached out and took the scale from Daddy. With a cry of pain Daddy swung round. When he saw her he went hopping mad. He jumped from one foot to the other and a string of curses flowed from his lips and a stream of tears from his eyes.

Leah grabbed Xuma and hugged him. Xuma smiled. The crowd of drinkers laughed and jeered at Daddy.

Xuma took the scale of beer from Leah's hand.

'I promised him. He would not show me the place unless I promised him.'

A smiled touched the side of Leah's face and one eyebrow went up. Her eyes lingered on Xuma for a little while, then she nodded. Xuma offered Daddy the scale. Daddy grabbed it and hurried out of the kitchen.

Xuma looked into Leah's eyes. Then they both burst out laughing.

'You got away,' Leah said.

He nodded.

'That's good. Did you hurt him?'

Xuma showed her his fist. 'He went to sleep.'

'Good again. But you must run when Joseph tells you. He knows the city.'

She patted Xuma's fist and smiled, 'You are a man. . . . Come, we will see if there is a place to talk.'

They went from room to room. But all the rooms were filled. Everywhere people were drinking.

'It is business,' Leah said.

She shook the leather money bag that was tied round her waist. It sounded full. 'This is power,' she said.

Xuma looked at her. Her eyes shone. Her face was slightly flushed. And the smile at the side of her face came and went. Her strong bosom rose and fell steadily. She caught him looking at her and laughed aloud. She looked stronger than ever.

'Questions again, heh?'

Her eyes twinkled.

They went on the verandah but it was the same there.

'It is business,' she said again and led him out into the street.

They walked up to the corner of the street.

'Have you had food?'

'No.'

'All right. When we finish this business you can go and have food with the teacher. She has come back. Good?'

'Yes,' he said.

'Tomorrow you can rest. And the day afterwards, if you still wish, you can go to the mines. . . . Tell me, have you a woman in the north?'

'No.'

'You want one here?'

'I will see.'

She smiled.

They stood on the corner and waited. Leah kept looking up the street that cut across the one where they stood.

After ten minutes a black policeman on a cycle came down and stopped.

'Hello,' Leah said.

'Hello,' the policeman said and looked at Xuma.

'He's all right,' Leah said.

'They will not come tonight,' the policeman said.

'Good.'

'But in the morning they will dig up your place and some others.'

'Ah. . . . Who are the others?'

'I do business with you,' the policeman said.

Leah smiled from the side of her mouth. She counted five one-pound notes from her leather bag and gave them to the policeman.

'You will not tell the others,' he said.

'I look after myself,' she replied and turned away.

The policeman rode away.

'Come,' Leah said and led the way back to the house.

Xuma caught up with her and took her arm.

'Will you tell the others?'

'What is it to you?' she said pulling away.

'You are a strange woman.'

'You are a fool! . . . Come! I have much to do.'

He followed her through the house, into the yard, and to the door at the far end of the yard. She knocked on the door and went in. Xuma followed her.

A young woman who sat eating looked up.

'This is Xuma,' Leah said.

Xuma smiled. The girl looked at him without smiling. This is the teacher, he thought.

'Give him food,' Leah said, 'and let him stay here. There is much to be done. They will come digging in the morning.'

'And tonight?' the girl asked.

'They will not come. So we will sell much and take the rest out later. I will call you. Maybe you and Xuma can go to the Bioscope when you've eaten, heh?'

Leah went out and shut the door behind her. Then she pushed her head back into the room again.

'Xuma, I'm not angry with you but don't be such a fool. If I tell the others the police will know we have been warned and that will be no good. Now eat. . . .'

Again she shut the door.

'Pull up a chair and sit down,' the girl said.

Xuma obeyed.

The girl got up and dished out some food for him. He watched her. She was beautiful. Like a smooth brown fresh flower. There was youth and strength in the grace of her body. Smooth, strong brown beauty. In her arms and in her legs and in the way she turned and the way she carried her head. And the softness of her voice was good. It was hard to stop looking at her.

She placed the food in front of him.

'You knocked the policeman down today,' she said.

He nodded.

'Why?'

'He struck me for no reason.'

'Why didn't you run?'

'Must a man run who has done nothing?'

Then she smiled at him for the first time. And it was good. Her teeth were beautiful, and her face broke into dimples. One on each cheek. Deep, beautiful things that wanted to be kissed. And her eyes were bright and deep when she smiled. He smiled back at her.

'You are not afraid?' she asked.

'I'm afraid of no man,' he declared with a note of boastfulness in his voice.

'Eat,' she said.

After a little while he looked up.

'What do they call you?'

'Eliza.'

'It's a good name.'

'Where are you from?' she asked.

'From the north.'

'Is it good?'

'It is very good.'

'Why did you leave?'

'There is no work. I will go in the mines here.'

She was silent and he thought of something to say, but there was nothing he could say. She was so beautiful. He looked at her hair and wanted to touch it. She looked up and saw him looking at her. She lowered her eyes again.

'How is the food?'

'It is good. Did you cook it?'

'Yes.'

Leah pushed her head through the door.

'She's beautiful, heh, Xuma?'

'Very beautiful.'

Leah laughed and shut the door with a bang.

'Will you drink?' Eliza asked.

'No.'

Eliza got up and cleared the things away. Xuma watched her. And silence settled over the room.

From outside the noise of the drinkers came faintly to them.

And every now and then they heard the voice of Leah silencing the drinkers when the din was too loud.

'Help me lift the machine, I will sew for a little,' Eliza said.

Xuma jumped up and grabbed the sewing machine. As he lifted it he felt sharp, painful stab in his left shoulder.

'You are hurt,' Eliza said.

'It is nothing,' he said.

'Let me see.'

'It is nothing.'

'Then let me see.'

'It is where that fool policeman struck me.'

'Sit here.'

She undid the shirt. There was a purple bruise where the policeman had struck him.

'You must put something on it,' she said.

She found the bottle of ointment and rubbed it on. Her fingers were soft and tender. He wished they could go on doing that.

'You are good,' he said. 'Good and beautiful.'

'You are lonely,' she said and laughed.

Again there was silence between them. But it was friendly. And the noises from outside seemed more friendly.

She gave him a cigarette and lit one for herself. She looked at his face and laughed.

'Is it the first time you've seen a woman smoke?'

'I've only seen the white women smoke.'

She threaded a needle and slowly the machine began to sing. It was a soft humming noise and he liked it.

'Tell me about your home,' she said, 'and your people.'

'It's far away,' he said. 'Between two hills and a river. And it's quiet. Not like here. When I think of it now I long for it. At one time we had many cattle but now there are only a few, and the land is poor. My father is there, and my brother and sister. They are younger than me.'

'And your mother?'

'She died.'

'Will you go back?'

'Yes.'

'And the city – do you like it?'

'I don't know.'

24

'Leah likes you. She talks a lot about you.'

'She is kind. But it's hard to understand her.'

'She's good, too.'

'You like her. What is she to you?'

'She's my mother's sister. When my mother died she looked after me and she sent me to school and now I'm a teacher. Did you go to school?'

'No. We have no school in our place.'

Eliza stopped sewing and covered the machine.

'Come, we will walk. I will take you where it is like the country.'

They left Malay Camp and walked away from the crowds and from the shouting and fighting and noise of the streets. And slowly these grew faint and distant till they were only a distant buzzing.

And after a time there was grass underfoot.

'It is peaceful here,' Eliza said.

'It is almost like the country,' Xuma said.

'When I get tired of the noise I come out here, sometimes,' she said.

'It is fresh here,' he said.

They sat down.

'There is the city,' Eliza said and pointed.

It lay slightly to the east. A mass of shadowy buildings and twinkling lights.

'It makes you lonely to look at it from here,' he said.

Eliza stretched herself and lay on her back with her arms pillowing her head.

'I like to look at the stars,' she said.

He turned and looked at her.

'You are beautiful.'

'You are lonely,' she said and laughed.

'Why do you say that?'

'Because it's true.'

He felt that there was something between them that he could not understand and that he could not push aside. He turned his head and looked westward. There he saw huge towering shadowy shapes that reared their heads to the sky. Huge round things that thinned as they rose, till only their points showed up against the sky. He pointed.

'What are those?'

Eliza raised herself and looked.

'Those are the mine-dumps. They are made of the sand that's dug out of the earth when the miners seek for gold. You will help to make those.'

'Just sand?'

'Yes,' she said wearily. 'Just sand.'

'It must have taken a long time.'

'It did. It took many years to make them all. And more are being made every day.'

'Have you been near them?'

'Yes.'

'What do they look like?'

'Like sand.'

'What colour?'

'White sand.'

'No black?'

'I didn't see any.'

'That's funny.'

'Why?'

'A mountain of white sand made by black men.'

'And white men too. . . . Come, we must go.'

She got up and stretched herself. Xuma sat staring at the mine-dumps. The moon suddenly appeared from behind a cloud. It was big and yellow and friendly. And in the sky the stars twinkled brightly. Xuma shifted his eyes from the mine-dumps to Eliza and longed for her.

'You are beautiful,' he said sternly.

'Come on,' she said.

'You do not like me.'

She looked at him strangely but said nothing. And in the moonlight it seemed that she smiled. A small smile from the side of her mouth. It reminded him of Leah.

She walked away. He got up and followed her. He took her arm and pulled her to him.

'You are very strong,' she said and laughed.

'Why don't you like me?'

Again there was that strange look in her eyes as she looked at him. And again she said nothing.

He pulled her close to him and held her tight. He felt the stiffness go out of her body and smiled.

Behind him lay the city and Malay Camp. And over there those mine-dumps made of white sand. And here it was quiet and peaceful and she was soft in his arms.

He took her chin in his big hand and raised her face. He smiled down into her eyes but there was no responding smile. A strange one, this. Like Leah. He reached down to kiss her.

Her body hardened again. She pushed him away.

'Don't!' she said, and it was like the cry of a child.

She turned her back on him and walked a little distance. Xuma stood and watched her.

'I am sorry,' she said without turning her head.

'It is nothing,' he said and walked away.

He took the path by which they had come. Once he stopped, turned and looked at the distant mine-dumps, then turned again and carried on.

She caught up with him as he neared Malay Camp and fell into step beside him. For a long time they walked in silence.

Then she raised her eyes and looked at him. She said:

'You are angry.'

'What is it to you?'

'I'm sorry,' she said, 'but you do not understand.'

He looked at her. There was sadness on her face. The anger left him. There was only a strange loneliness in his breast now.

'I'm not angry,' he said.

They walked in silence for the rest of the way. . . .

All that night people drank at Leah's place. When Xuma and Eliza returned the place was even more crowded than it had been when they left.

Old Ma Plank still sat in the same place in the yard. Behind her were two empty vats, and in front of her was a half-empty one. And the yard was packed with people.

The thin coloured woman who had had the horrors in the afternoon, now had another vat in another corner of the yard, and she was also selling. Xuma was surprised to see that she was sober.

In the house too, every room was crowded with men and women drinking. There were many coloured women with their arms round black men. But only one or two coloured men.

One thin, hard-faced coloured woman came and put her arms round Xuma's neck and said:

'Buy me a drink, daddy, and then we can go to sleep. Only half-a-crown.'

Eliza left him and went into the room. Xuma went into the yard again. Leah was leaning against a wall talking to a group of men and laughing at the top of her voice. Her face was flushed and she was mocking the men with her eyes.

'Xuma!' It was the voice of old Ma Plank.

He went over to her.

'Sit here, my son,' she said, and made a place for him on the bench beside her. 'I have much money and I want you to take some of it and keep it to give to Leah. These people are drunk and there may be some fighting, and I'm old.'

She gave him a wad of notes and patted his arms. Then she pushed him away. He smiled. Her voice was sweet and motherly. It reminded him of his old mother.

'Come up! Come up! you sons of dogs! Come and choke your guts with drink!' Ma Plank yelled and there was nothing motherly in her voice.

Xuma looked at her and laughed. She winked roguishly at him and her leathery old face creased in a naughty smile.

'Come dogs!' she yelled. 'Where are your shillings!'

Xuma walked away.

'Here he is, the bastard!'

Xuma turned. Something flashed past his face. He stepped back.

'That's for stealing my woman,' Dladla shouted.

He brandished a knife. Behind him were two other men with knives. Xuma felt blood trickling down the side of his face.

Dladla laughed and cut the air with his knife. The two behind him stepped closer. Xuma stepped back feeling for something hard and solid.

'Take this,' a woman's voice said and pushed a club into his hands. It was Lena, the thin coloured woman who had had the horrors. Xuma raised the club.

'Come,' he said.

'Leave that Dladla for me!' Leah's voice said.

Dladla stepped back and turned his head. Xuma raised the club and took a step towards Dladla.

'No! He's mine. Watch the other two.

She came forward slowly, arms akimbo, a smile on the one side of her face. People moved back, away from the little group in the centre. One of Dladla's henchmen turned his eyes to Leah. Xuma struck. The man collapsed without a sound. The other one made a dash for the gate but was caught by a tall man who had just come in. The tall man grabbed his throat and shook him.

'My name is J. P. Williamson and I'm going to kill you son-ofabitch,' the tall man roared.

'Johannes!' Lena, the thin coloured woman shouted.

Without loosening his grip the big man looked at her.

'Don't kill him, you'll go to jail,' Lena shouted.

'I'll crush the sonofabitch!' Johannes roared.

'No!' Lena shouted and there was authority in her voice.

With a grunt Johannes released the man. The man slid to the ground and lay still.

'If you come nearer I'll knife you,' Dladla said stepping back from Leah.

'Another one,' Johannes roared stepping forward.

'He's mine,' Leah said.

Johannes stepped back.

'Don't come any nearer woman!'

Leah took another step. Dladla slashed out. He missed her. She grabbed his arm and pushed it away. He strained to bring the knife down on her shoulder. But Leah held him like a vice.

'Try harder,' she whispered and hit him in the face with her forehead.

A trickle of blood flowed from his nose. Veins stood out on his forehead and neck as he strained to bring the knife down.

Locked in the dreadful tug, they swayed from side to side. Desperately, Dladla tried to trip her up. She snorted. Then slowly she pushed his arm back. Back. Back. Back. Beads of sweat showed on his forehead. His face twisted with pain. There was a harsh crack and Dladla went limp. The knife slipped from his fingers.

Leah left him and he collapsed in a heap. She looked down and spat. Then she raised her heel and brought it down on his face.

'No!' Xuma said.

She looked at him, half smiled, then turned away.

'Take the dirt away,' she said.

Eliza took Xuma's arm.

'Come, I will wash off the blood on your face.'

He went with her to the room. She got a basin of water and bathed his face.

'It is not deep,' she said, 'but we must get it fixed or it will bleed more. . . . Come!'

'It is nothing,' he said.

Impatiently she dragged him out. . . .

They returned an hour later. They had found a doctor and Xuma's face had been stitched up.

There were no people in the yard. Nor in the house. They had all gone. Only big Johannes and Lena were still there. And everywhere the stench of beer was strong.

'Is it bad?' Leah asked.

Xuma shook his head.

'Johannes works in the mines,' Leah said. 'He will help you, heh Johannes?'

'My name is J. P. Williamson,' Johannes replied, 'I will help him!'

Daddy, supported by Ma Plank, came in. He had been sleeping and he was sobering.

Xuma looked at Johannes. He looked like a coloured man but he spoke and behaved like any of the others. And the thin coloured woman loved him, one could see that.

Leah looked at Xuma, then at Eliza, and laughed.

'He has lost much blood,' Eliza said.

'Let him sleep,' Leah said. 'You will help us to take out the tins and clear up the place so that things are right when the police come in the morning.'

Eliza nodded. Xuma and Leah and Eliza went into the yard and to the room. Leah sat down and looked at Xuma.

'You will sleep here. Eliza will sleep in the house. . . . How is it with you?'

'It is all right.'

'Do you want food?'

'No.'

'Drink?'

'No.'

'That one?' Leah nodded in Eliza's direction.

'Don't be foolish,' Eliza said.

Xuma was silent. Leah sighed and laughed. Xuma remembered the money Ma Plank had given him. He took it out and gave it to Leah. She got up, slapped him on the back and went to the door. Again she nodded in Eliza's direction, 'That one likes you but she's a fool. It is going to school. She likes you but she wants one who can read books and dresses like the white folks and speaks the language of the whites and wear the little bit of cloth they call a tie. Take her by force or you will be a fool too.'

With another laugh she went out. Xuma watched Eliza.

'Is that so?'

She would not look at him.

'Your bed is made,' she said. 'You can sleep now.'

She went out without answering his question.

FOUR

Johannes drunk and Johannes sober were two different people. The one was loud and boastful and arrogant and told the world that he was J. P. Williamson and he would crush any son-ofabitch. He joyed in fights and in his great strength and dared anybody at any time. The other was quiet and retiring and soft spoken. Gentle as a lamb and seemingly ashamed of his great size and great strength. And almost afraid of looking at anybody and always just too ready to step aside, and very hard to provoke.

And on this early Monday morning Johannes was sober and his face was serious. And his brows were bunched in the manner of a man who broods a great deal.

Every now and then Xuma looked at him. But Johannes kept plodding on with his head lowered. There were so many questions Xuma wanted to ask him. Xuma had tried. But he had said yes or no in a soft voice that held a tinge of sadness, and it was hard to speak to him. Xuma wondered what the mines would really be like.

'The streets are empty now,' Xuma said, remembering how crowded they had been on Saturday.

'Yes,' Johannes replied.

They looked unfamiliar, so empty, Johannes thought, but he said nothing. As though they should not be like that. Long and wide and empty. Street after street. And the shops too. Just windows without people looking into them. And the awful humming quiet over all. And the faint lights from the street lamps. Everything looked so unfamiliar like this. Like death. And Johannes did not like that. He did not like the thought of death. . . .

'It is so quiet now,' Xuma said. 'I like it. I do not like it when it is so crowded and there are people around, like on Saturday.'

'Hmm,' Johannes grunted. But to himself he said, 'I like it when there are crowds.'

'What?'

'Nothing.'

'I thought you spoke,' Xuma said looking at him.

'No.'

And again they walked in silence for a long time. Up the empty streets and down the empty streets with tall sleeping buildings on either side and goods and clothes in shop windows.

But not a car anywhere and not a person anywhere. The city of gold sleeping and they were the only two waking, walking things in it. It is like a dead place, Johannes thought, and I do not like dead places.

It is beautiful like this, Xuma thought, beautiful and peaceful.

He likes it, Johannes thought, but I like people. Not just empty streets and dead buildings. People. People.

He's a strange man, Xuma thought; yesterday he was loud and boastful and now he's so quiet you can hardly hear his voice when he speaks. I wonder what it will be like in the mines, Xuma thought. He had asked Johannes but Johannes had not replied. He tried again:

'How is it in the mines?'

Johannes looked at him with puzzled eyes.

'I have never been in a mine,' Xuma explained.

Still the frown of puzzlement showed on Johannes' face. Xuma wondered whether Johannes understood why he asked and spoke again:

'I do not fear the work. It is just that I want to understand and know what to do.'

'You will understand. It is not hard to learn.'

Johannes pursed his lips and looked away. He hated the empty streets. He hated the sound their feet made. It increased the emptiness of the streets. And speaking made it even worse.

Xuma opened his mouth to speak, looked at Johannes' face, then changed his mind.

They left Johannesburg behind them, not far behind. It was just behind the little rising they had topped and they could still see the taller buildings if they looked.

And in front of them were the towering peaks of the

33

mine-dumps. Xuma looked at them. They looked ordinary and commonplace now, not as they had looked on Saturday night when he had watched them with Eliza. Then there had been something beautiful and faraway and grand about them. Now they were just ordinary mountains of sand and he did not like them.

'There are some men who are going to the mines,' Johannes said and pointed. Xuma looked.

To the left of them, and a little below them a smooth macadamised road ran. And round its left bend a stream of men marched. Morning had not quite broken and it was hard to make them out as anything but a body of marching men.

'There are many,' Xuma said.

'Yes.'

'Where do they come from?'

'From the compound,' Johannes said and sat on the grass. Xuma seated himself beside Johannes and watched the column of men approaching.

'The compound is in Langlaagte,' Johannes said softly. 'All the mine boys must live in compounds.'

'And you?' Xuma asked.

For a short spell there was silence. The long column drew near but was still a great distance away. Johannes pointed at the column:

'They are not of the city, they come from the farms and some are from the land of the Portuguese and others are from Rhodesia. The white man fetched them. And those that are fetched must live in the compounds. It is the law here. But I came to the city like you and I am the boss boy for a white man so I do not stay in the compounds. They do not take many boys from the city for they do not like them.'

'And will they take me?'

Johannes nodded and began to chew a piece of grass.

The column drew near. Johannes got up and stretched himself.

'Come, we will walk with them.'

Xuma followed him down the slight incline and together they waited by the roadside.

In front of the long column marched an induna, a mine policeman, whose duty it was to keep order among the boys. And

34

flanking the column on either side, ten yards from each other, walked others. The indunas all carried knob-kerries and assagais. The column of men hummed as they marched.

Xuma watched curiously.

'Why do those others carry assagais?'

'It is the law,' Johannes said.

The column drew abreast of them.

'Morning!' Johannes called.

'Morning, Williamson!' the induna in front yelled. 'How is it in the city?'

'Like always,' Johannes replied.

They fell into step with the marching column but remained on the side of the road.

Xuma looked at the faces of the marching men. There was little expression on any. Then he saw an elderly man smiling at him. He returned the smile. The elderly man greeted him with his hand.

'Who is that one?' Xuma asked Johannes.

Johannes looked then shook his head. Again Xuma looked at the elderly man.

'Who is your friend, Williamson!' the induna in front yelled above the dull thud of the marching feet.

'He is called Xuma!' Johannes replied.

'Ho Xuma!' the induna yelled.

'Ho!' Xuma replied and turned his eyes back to the elderly man. There was something in the eyes of the elderly man, a message of some kind but Xuma could not understand it and shook his head.

'Is he going to the mines, Williamson?' yelled the induna.

'The Red One is the one he will work for.'

The road turned and when it straightened again they could see the mine gates in front of them.

In the east the first streaks of the morning sun began to show. The dull thud of the heavy boots of the marching men rumbled on. A trail of settling dust showed in the wake of the column. And above it all rose the humming of the marching men.

The gates opened and the men marched through. A group of white men came out of a low smoky building and watched the men marching past. The column turned to the left and disappeared behind a mine-dump and a few buildings. The sound of the tramping feet faded.

The sound of tramping feet came back. But this time from the right. Xuma turned his head. There was another column of men. He looked at Johannes.

'The night-shift,' Johannes said.

They marched out through the gate, flanked by indunas and led by indunas. They looked just like the column that had gone in, but there was something else to them. Something that was foreign to the column that had marched in. Xuma looked closely to see what it was. But it was nothing he could see. It was there but he couldn't see it.

The column disappeared round the bend of the road. The sound of tramping feet grew less, and faded.

'Wait here,' Johannes said and went up to the gate. An induna stepped forward. Johannes raised his arms and held them extended. The induna felt his pockets. Johannes stepped past and disappeared behind a low building.

Two white men on cycles came round the bend of the road. The induna opened the gate. The white men cycled in. Then three cars followed each other and also went in through the gates.

Johannes returned.

'The Red One has not come yet, we will wait here.'

An explosion, followed by a rumbling noise, came from somewhere behind the gates. Xuma jumped.

'It is a strange place,' he said.

'You will learn to know it.'

A cycle swept round the bend of the road and raced towards the gates.

'That is my white man,' Johannes said.

The white man applied the brakes and his cycle skidded for a full ten yards before it came to a stop. The man got off and laughed. He was as tall and broad as Johannes. But he was younger and looked stronger. There were lines of laughter on his face and his eyes twinkled merrily.

'Ho there, Johannes,' the white man said, 'who's looking after the boys if you are here?'

'I have seen them. It is all right.'

'Bless my soul, Johannes, you are sober!'

The white man tapped Johannes on the chest and laughed.

'The police smashed everything,' Johannes said and the shadow of a smile crossed his face.

The white man slapped his thighs and laughed. Then suddenly he stopped and looked at Xuma.

'Hi, Chris!' one of the white men from the door of the smoky room called.

'Coming!' Chris shouted back.

He turned his eyes back to Xuma and examined him closely. He bent his head forward and raised his chin.

'And who is this?'

'He is called Xuma,' Johannes said.

'Yabo?' Chris asked, cocking his head.

'Yabo,' Xuma said and smiled.

The white man returned his smile. And then suddenly his fist shot out and smacked hard against Xuma's chest. Xuma's eyes blazed. Instinctively he stepped back and raised his arms, both hands bunched into great fists.

Quickly the white man held up his hands. But his eyes twinkled.

'Sorry Xuma, but I wanted to see if you are a man,' he patted Johannes' shoulder affectionately, 'this one is a woman, only when he is drunk is he a man. All right?'

Chris held out his hand. Doubtfully Xuma shook it. Chris searched in his pocket and found a packet of cigarettes. He gave it to Johannes, 'Share it with Xuma. And you can take him inside, Johannes, I will speak to the Red One.'

'Hi, Chris!' the man from the smoky shack shouted again.

'Coming!' Chris yelled and walked to the gate.

'White man!' Johannes called.

Chris stopped and turned.

'Tell that one at the gate Xuma can go in.'

'All right,' Chris said.

He entered the gate and spoke to the induna at the gate then joined the other white men at the smoky shack.

'Come,' said Johannes to Xuma. 'It is all right now.'

'But where is the one with the red head? You said I would work for him.'

'If that one says it is all right it is so. He is the great friend of the Red One. Come.'

Johannes led the way. They went through the gate. The induna grabbed Xuma by the arm. Xuma jerked away.

'He must search you,' Joannes said. 'It is the law.'

The induna pushed Xuma's arms up. Xuma stretched them as he had seen Johannes do. The induna felt his pockets then nodded. He did not really search. But it was the law.

Johannes smiled and lowered his eyes as Xuma looked at him. Suddenly Xuma smiled too. They moved away.

'I like your white man,' Xuma said.

'He is good,' Johannes said.

'He is a Dutchman?' Xuma asked.

'Yes. Your one comes from over the seas. This way.'

Johannes led him to a little glass window with a hole in it. Johannes tapped on the sill. A white man appeared.

'Yes?'

'There is a new one,' Johannes said.

'Your gang?'

'No. For the Red One. Boss boy.'

'The Red One has not come.'

'My white man said so.'

'You mean your boss.'

'My white man.'

The man at the window stared at Johannes. Johannes returned the stare. The man at the window cursed and turned his eyes to Xuma.

'What is your name?'

'Xuma.'

'Where's your pass?'

Xuma gave him the pass. The man went away. After some time he returned with a stiff piece of blue paper. He pushed it to Xuma.

'Guard it well,' the man said.

Xuma took the stiff piece of paper and looked at it. He could not read what was written on it; it said:

PASS NATIVE XUMA
GANG LEADER FOR MR PADDY O'SHEA

'And my pass?' Xuma asked.

'After work,' the man at the window said and turned away.

Xuma followed Johannes round the building to where a group of men were loading trucks with sand and pushing the trucks away. Two indunas and a white man were in charge of this gang of about fifty men.

'You will work here today,' Johannes told him.

Johannes took him to the white man and told the white man he was the new boss boy of the Red One.

Xuma didn't like the white one. His eyes told you he was one of those white men who liked to kick you and push you and curse you.

When he had finished explaining, Johannes pulled Xuma to one side. 'This one is no good but you will only be here today. But it will be all right. Do not answer him back if he angers you. That one over there will take you when it is time to eat. I must go now, Xuma. . . . Good luck.'

Xuma watched Johannes walk away. Watched him get to a group of men who were waiting at the gate of a cage. One of the men gave Johannes a cap that had a lamp tied to it. Johannes lit the lamp and put the cap on his head. Then Johannes waved the men into the cage and followed them in. A whistle blew. The cage moved downward till it was out of sight and there was a vacant hole where the cage had been. Xuma had known it would happen. Yet it shocked him. His heart pounded. His hands were clammy with sweat.

'Hi, you!'

Xuma jumped. He looked at the white man. The white man's eyes blazed with anger.

'Push that!'

Xuma looked at the white man, then at the loaded truck, then up the steep incline along which the lines lay, and then back at the white man. The induna nearest Xuma protested under his breath. A few men further away grumbled in their throats.

'He does not know how,' one man whispered.

'It is the work of two men,' another whispered.

'Shut up!' the white man roared.

The whispers and grumbling stopped.

Why is he angry with me, Xuma wondered. Then slowly he

walked over to the truck. The two men who had intended to push it stepped aside. Xuma braced himself against the side of the truck and looked at the white man. There was a strange light in the white man's eyes. And just behind the white man he could see Johannes' white man and another. And the other one had red hair. Yes, it was the Red One. And they too, had strange looks on their faces. But not the same as this other one who had told him to push the truck.

'Go on!' the white man roared.

Xuma pushed. The top part of the truck moved but the wheels remained in the same place.

'Lower!' a man whispered fiercely.

The end he had pushed kept moving forward, the truck began to tilt. It was tipping over, Xuma realized, and pulled it. The wheels moved backward but the truck kept tilting forward. If he didn't do something quickly the thing would tip over and the sand would be thrown over the line.

Xuma saw the look on the white man's face. The brightness of his eyes and the smile of victory on his lips.

'Pig!' Xuma whispered and braced himself. He pushed his left leg forward till the axle of the wheels pushed against his shin, then he leaned back and pulled with all the massive strength in his body. He felt the skin of his leg cracking and hot blood running down to his ankle. His jaws hardened and he pulled harder. Suddenly the truck righted itself. Beads of sweat showed on his forehead. A heavy sigh burst from the crowd of watching men.

Xuma smiled though his leg pained him, leaned down and found a balance, and pushed. Slowly the truck moved up the tracks. Here and there a man laughed with a note of nervousness in his laughter. It is easy if you know how, Xuma thought.

'Xuma!'

Xuma stopped and turned. It was Johannes' white man.

Johannes' white man spoke and two other men came and carried on with the pushing of the truck.

'Come here,' Chris called.

Xuma took a deep breath. His heart pounded furiously. His leg burned and there was a tightness round his forehead.

Chris took his arm and Xuma could feel the white man's fingers tremble. And there was a brightness in the white man's eye that told of a lust for battle. Xuma smiled.

40

'It is all right.'

'You are strong, Xuma,' Chris said, looking at the white man who had told Xuma to push the truck. 'Here is the Red One, he's a strong one too. Are you hurt?'

'Only a little in my leg,' Xuma said.

'Let me see?'

Xuma pulled his trousers up and showed the gash.

'The induna will take you to have it bandaged,' Chris said.

Xuma looked at the Red One and did not like him. His eyes were hard and brooding. No laughter in them like in Chris's. And his mouth was hard. A just one but a hard one, Xuma decided.

He was a little shorter than Chris but broader. His chin pushed out and his eyes were blue. And because of his mass of red hair he was called the Red One.

For a long time he stared at Xuma without saying a word, then he turned to the white man who had told Xuma to push the truck:

'This is my boy, and if I were you I shouldn't try that again.'

His voice was deep and low. He turned to Xuma:

'I cannot make the click in your name come right so I'll call you Zuma. All right?'

Xuma nodded. He wondered if the Red One ever smiled.

Chris smiled at Xuma, and the two white men walked away. Somewhere the five-thirty whistle blew. . . .

For Xuma the day was strange. Stranger than any day he had ever known. There was the rumbling noise and the shouting and the explosions and the tremblings of the earth. And always the shouting indunas driving the men on to work. And over all those was the bitter eyes and hardness of the white man who had told him to push the truck when he did not know how.

But these were not the worst. These were confusing and frightening. It was the strangeness of it all that terrified him. And the look in the eyes of the other men who worked with him. He had seen that look before when he was at home on the farms. He had seen it when he herded his cattle and when a dog came among the sheep and barked. The eyes of these men were like the eyes of the sheep that did not know where to run when the dog barked. It was this that frightened him.

And when a lorry came the men jumped out of the road and ran like the sheep. Over all this the induna was like a shepherd with a spear. And the white man sat with folded arms.

With another he had pushed the loaded truck up the incline. The path was narrow on which they had to walk and it was difficult to balance well. And the white man had shouted, 'Hurry up!' And the induna had taken up the shout. And one little truck after another, loaded with fine wet white sand, was pushed up the incline to where a new mine-dump was being born.

But as fast as they moved the sand, so fast did the pile grow. A truck load would go and another would come from the bowels of the earth. And another would go and another would come. And another. And yet another. So it went on all day long. On and on and on and on.

And men gasped for breath and their eyes turned red and beads of sweat stood on their foreheads and the muscles in their arms hardened with pain as they fought the pile of fine wet sand.

But the sand remained the same. A truck would come from the heart of the earth. A truck would go up to build the mine-dump. Another would come. Another would go. . . . All day long. . . .

And for all their sweating and hard breathing and for the redness of their eyes and the emptiness of their stare there would be nothing to show. In the morning the pile had been so big. Now it was the same. And the mine-dump did not seem to grow either.

It was this that frightened Xuma. This seeing of nothing for a man's work. This mocking of a man by the sand that was always wet and warm; by the mine-dump that would not grow; by the hard eyes of the white man who told them to hurry up.

It made him feel desperate and anxious. He worked feverishly. Straining his strength behind the loaded truck and running behind the empty truck and looking carefully to see if the dump had grown any bigger, and watching the sand from the earth to see if it had grown less. But it was the same. The same all the time. No change.

Only the startling and terrifying noises around. And the whistles blowing. And the hissing and the explosions from the bowels of the earth. And these things beat against his brain till his eyes reddened like the eyes of the other men.

When the whistle blew for them to stop for food, one of the men who had been filling the trucks called Xuma.

'I am Nana,' the man told him, 'you will eat with me.'

They found a shaded spot and sat on the ground. Everywhere men found places for themselves and ate their food. All the men had the same kind of little tins. In each tin was a hunk of mealie meal porridge cooked into a hardened chunk, a piece of meat, and a piece of very coarse compound bread.

Nana divided his food and gave Xuma half.

Xuma wiped his brow and leaned against the corrugated wall of the smoky shack. To the left was a mine-dump, big and overpowering. To the right of it they had been dumping sand all morning without seeing anything for it. Nana followed his eyes.

'It takes a long time,' Nana said.

'Is it like this every day?'

'Every day.'

'It is a strange place.'

'It is hard when you are new, but it is not so bad. With a new one it is thus: First there is a great fear, for you work and you work and there is nothing to see for it. And you look and you look and the more you look the more there is nothing to see. This brings fear. But tomorrow you think, well, there will be nothing to look for and you do not look so much. The fear is less then. And the day after you look even less, and after that even less, and in the end you do not look at all. Then all the fear goes. It is so.'

'But the eyes of the men . . .' Xuma protested.

'The eyes of the men?'

'Yes. I watched them, they are like the eyes of sheep.'

Nana looked at Xuma and smiled. A smile that softened his face and made gentle creases round his mouth.

'Are we not all sheep that talk,' Nana said.

For a spell they ate in silence. When they had finished Nana stretched himself full-length on the ground and closed his eyes. One by one the other men did it too, till all were stretched full-length on the ground.

'Do it too,' Nana said, 'it gives your body rest.'

Xuma obeyed.

'Better, heh?'

'Yes.'

'Now make your body go soft all over.'

Somewhere a man began to hum softly. Others joined in. A low, soft monotonous hum, it was. Xuma joined in. It made him feel easier. He could feel the stiffness leaving his body. The aching of his back became less. He closed his eyes.

The noise and hissings and explosions seemed subdued by the humming. Xuma opened his eyes and looked at the sky. It was blue up there. And at home in the country it would be green now and there would be cattle on the hillside. His eyes suddenly felt wet. With the back of his hand he rubbed them vigorously.

'How is it underground?' he asked loudly.

Nana turned his head and looked at him.

'Some like it, some do not.'

The whistle blew. The half hour was up.

The men got up, stretched themselves, and slowly went back to their work.

Trucks were loaded with fine wet sand. Men pushed the trucks away and emptied them. Other trucks came up from the bowls of the earth, also loaded with fine wet warm sand. . . . So it went on. . . .

When the sun was slanting far to the west the men who had gone underground that morning came up. Streams of men coming from the bowels of the earth.

Xuma watched them coming and shading their eyes against the light.

'Is it dark underground?' he asked Nana.

Nana looked at him and laughed. 'Did you think there was a sun?'

Xuma swung his spade with force. It crunched against the fine wet warm sand. For the latter part of the day he had been taken off pushing the trucks and had been loading them. He flung the spadeful of sand into the truck.

'Xuma!'

Johannes was pushing through the crowd of men. Xuma looked at the white man who was in charge of them and waited.

'Ho!' Johannes said. 'How goes it?'

'This one is strong,' Nana said as Johannes joined them.

'Williamson!' the white man in charge shouted.

44

'The Red One wants him,' Johannes said over his shoulder.

Xuma looked up quickly when he heard Johannes' voice. The note of boastfulness was back in it. Yes, the arrogant light was there in his eyes too. But he was underground, Xuma thought.

'You should have come to me,' the white man said heatedly.

'What for?' Johannes sneered.

The white man walked over to Johannes.

'Who are you speaking to?'

'You?' Johannes said and looked the white man in the face.

They stood staring at each other. The white man's face was red with anger. There was a reckless smile on Johannes' lips that seemed to say, 'My name is J. P. Williamson and I will crush you sonofabitch.' Then the white man turned and walked away.

'Your cheek is going to get you into trouble, kaffir.'

'Come, Xuma,' Johannes said and laughed.

Xuma flung the spade away and followed him. Johannes took him to the shed of the mine doctor. Chris and Paddy were there.

'Hello, Xuma!' Chris exclaimed. 'How did it go?'

'Well,' Xuma replied.

Paddy, the Red One, was silent.

'Come here, Xuma,' the doctor said.

Xuma stripped and lay on the long table. Chris and Paddy and Johannes watched while the doctor examined him. When he had finished the doctor told Xuma to dress.

'Strong as an ox,' the doctor said, 'but it's still irregular for him to go down tomorrow.'

'Johannes will nurse him,' Chris said.

'That may be, but you two are always breaking the rules. One day you are going to get into trouble. . . . But what say you, Ireland?'

'He'll be all right,' Paddy said shortly.

'Do you want to go underground, Xuma?' the doctor asked.

'Yes!' Xuma said eagerly.

The doctor laughed. 'All right.'

They went out.

'Xuma.'

Xuma looked at Paddy and waited.

'Go and wash then come back to me before you go. All right?'

Xuma nodded.

The two white men went to the little shack where the other white men were. Johannes led the way to the washing place for the mine boys.

Johannes pushed a few men out of the way, 'My name is J. P. Williamson,' he roared.

Xuma shook his head and followed. The men made places for them. They washed then went out. Xuma waited while Johannes went into the shack to call Paddy. When they came, both Paddy and Chris had washed.

'Get the cycles,' Chris told Johannes.

'Come,' Paddy said to Xuma.

Xuma and Paddy walked to the gate. Chris followed a little distance behind. And Johannes brought up the rear, pushing the two cycles. The sun was sinking. Round the bend of the road a column of men, flanked and led by indunas, came marching to the gate. They made the dull tramp-tramp-tramp-tramp sound of marching feet. They entered the gates and disappeared to the left. From the right a column marched out on their way to the compound.

'If you work for me I want no nonsense,' Paddy said. 'It is hard underground, but if you are a good worker it will be all right. You will look after the other boys. You will make them work. That is your job. But to be a good leader you must be a good worker. If your work is no good you will be a bad boss boy.

'Sometimes men will be lazy then you must use your fist and you must kick them. It is so here, that's why I want a strong man.

'But to be strong is not enough, you must lead. And men will only follow a fearless one. You must be that one. There will be fifty men under you. Some will try to see if you are soft. You will have to crush them with your fist or you are no good. Some will be jealous because you are new and are put over them and you do not know the work. You must deal with them and you must learn the work quickly.

'If you are good, I will be your friend. If you are not, I will be your enemy. That is all my indaba with you. Is it wise?'

'It is wise,' Xuma replied.

'All right.'

Paddy shot out his hand. Xuma shook it. The grip was the grip of two strong men.

'Have you money?'

'No, baas.'

'Don't call me baas. Here.'

Paddy pulled a wad of notes out of his pocket and gave Xuma one.

'I have some old things underground. You can wear them in the morning. That is all.'

They waited for the other pair. Then the two white men got on their cycles and rode off.

'Don't get too drunk, Johannes!' Chris shouted back.

Johannes waved and laughed.

'Come,' Johannes said.

They set off for Malay Camp.

FIVE

When they got to Leah's place a group of women were just leaving. Leah was standing at the gate, watching them go, arms akimbo and a twisted smile on the side of her face.

'Ho! Xuma,' she said. 'How did the work go?'

'It was all right.'

'Ho! Johannes.'

'That's me, Leah. My name's J. P. Williamson and I'll crush any sonofabitch! Just show him to me, Leah, my sister, and I'll crush him for you. My name is J. P. . . .'

Leah laughed and patted Xuma's arm.

'Again. Where did he get the drink from? When he has no money he comes here. When he has money he drinks elsewhere. Where did you go, Xuma?'

'We came straight here.'

'Bah!' Leah said.

'He was like that when he came out of the mines,' Xuma said.

Leah looked at Xuma, then at Johannes.

'It is so, sister, 's true 's God. My white man had whisky underground and he gave me some.'

'And you liked it?' she asked, looking at Xuma.

'It was not so bad.'

'But you look unhappy.'

'I'm not.'

Leah clicked her tongue.

'Don't lie to me! I told you you are like a baby with people.'

'Who were those women?' Xuma asked, looking away.

Leah cocked her eyebrow and smiled.

'They are the Stockvelt. They are all women who sell beer. And if one is arrested they all come together and collect money among themselves and bail out the arrested one. They are here to collect money for those who were arrested yesterday. But the police know about this and there will not be any fines.'

'I see,' Xuma said staring down the street.

Leah watched him for a minute than turned to Johannes:

'Go inside, your woman is there but she is sober. And tell Ma Plank to prepare food.'

Johannes went.

'Let us sit down,' Leah said.

They sat on a long wooden bench that was propped back on the pavement against the wall.

'In your heart you still think it is my fault those others are in jail. You think I should have told them the police were coming to dig on Sunday. Heh?'

'It is nothing to me. This is your business.'

'But in your heart you blame me.'

'Who am I to blame you.'

'But you do. I saw it in your eyes just now when I told you about the women. Heh?'

Xuma turned his head and looked at Leah. For a long time they looked at each other.

'Yes, I do,' Xuma said.

'Ah! And it makes you unhappy. Why?'

'You have been good to me.'

'And so?'

Xuma shook his head.

'I don't know! I don't know! Let me be, woman!'

Leah smiled and stared into space. For a long time they sat like that.

Around them the street was alive. People moved up and down. Children played in the gutters, and picked up dirty orange peels and ate them.

The pulsating motion of Malay Camp at night was everywhere. Warm and intense and throbbing.

People sang.

People cried.

People fought.

People loved.

People hated.
Others were sad.
Others gay.
Others with friends.
Others lonely.
Some died.
Some were born . . .
'You say you don't
know. I know, Xuma, I
know.'

She looked at him and
there was the shadow of
a smile on her lips but her
eyes were serious. 'I know,'

she whispered. Then she pulled herself together and her voice changed:

'Listen to me Xuma. I will try again to make you understand.
In the city it is like this: all the time you are fighting. Fighting.
Fighting! When you are asleep and when you are awake. And you
look only after yourself. If you do not you are finished. If you are
soft everyone will spit in your face. They will rob you and cheat
you and betray you. So, to live here, you must be hard. Hard as a
stone. And money is your best friend. With money you can buy a
policeman. With money you can buy somebody to go to jail for
you. That is how it is, Xuma. It may be good, it may be bad, but
there it is. And to live one must see it. Where you come from it
isn't so. But here it is so.'

Again there was a long silence between them. The stars came out
and twinkled brightly in the sky. The moon came up, and chasing
the Milky Way, travelled eastward.

Rosita who lived across the way turned on her gramophone and
came on her verandah swaying her broad hips.

'Hello!' she called across to Leah.

Leah looked up, startled. Xuma too, was startled.

'We must go in,' Leah said. 'Food will be ready.'

'My white man gave me a pound,' Xuma said. 'Will you take
some of it for my food and my sleeping here?'

Leah got up. She stared down at him then turned away.

'No. You can pay me when you get paid properly,' she said
gruffly. 'Come.'

50

They went in.

A fire, made in a paraffin tin with holes in the side, stood in the centre of the kitchen. And around it, on the floor, sat Ma Plank, Daddy, a man who was a stranger to Xuma, the pale fat one called Drunk Liz, Lena the thin coloured woman, Johannes, and another woman who was also a stranger.

Only Daddy, Johannes and Drunk Liz were not sober.

'Ah, Xuma, my boy,' Daddy said, 'you are going to get me a drink, are you not? You promised me.'

'He's drunk,' Ma Plank said, digging Daddy in the ribs.

'Sonofabitch Xuma,' Johannes said.

'Shut up, Johannes!' Lena said.

'Sonofabitch,' Johannes said and rubbed the knuckles of his fist across his face.

Lena smiled tolerantly. She looked very pretty when she was sober. Xuma looked at her and found it hard to believe that she was the same person he had seen getting the horrors on Saturday.

'This one is Samwell,' Leah said pointing to the strange man. 'And that one over there is Maisy.'

Xuma nodded at the man and woman. The woman was young but not pretty. But her eyes always laughed and this made men look at her.

'Eliza is not here,' Ma Plank said, looking at Xuma.

'Hold your tongue, old woman!' Leah said.

Ma Plank laughed. 'But there are others here, heh Xuma? I may be old, but an experienced horse is good too, not so, Xuma?'

'Hold your tongue and give the man food,' Leah said.

Laughing, Ma Plank got up and began to dish up. She dished for everybody.

Xuma kept looking at Lena.

'She's a strange one,' Leah said, following his eyes. 'She has a son who goes to school and will be a teacher soon; and her daughter has a fine house and a husband who looks like a white man. But here she is, working in a black woman's shebeen for a little beer and food. Strange, heh?'

Lena lowered her head. Her eyes filled with tears. Quickly Leah went round to her and took Lena in her arms as though she were a child. Lena clung to Leah. Leah rocked her from side to side and spoke soothingly:

'I did not mean to upset you, little one. I'm sorry. It is nothing. Nothing. Stop crying. You know I love you. It is only this sour tongue of mine that makes me say things. There now, wipe those tears.'

'It is not my children's fault,' Lena said through her tears. 'They have tried to help me. . . .'

'There, there. . . . Don't tell them, it is not their business. It is all my fault. The devil must have been in me to mock you. Forgive?'

Leah's face was soft and motherly as she looked down at the little coloured woman. Lena nodded and pressed her arm.

'Good. . . . Now eat, all of you.'

Johannes flung his arm round Lena's neck and pulled her towards him. Lena tried to resist but she was like a feather in his hands. The others laughed as he picked her up and propped her on his lap.

'Why did you do it?' Xuma asked, looking at Leah.

'You wanted to know,' Leah said.

'You are hard,' he said and there was anger in his voice.

Leah shrugged and turned away.

Conversation buzzed round the room. Xuma finished his food and left the room. He felt dissatisfied and unhappy suddenly. He went on to the verandah and watched the street. He listened to the noises of the street and tried to identify them. He wondered where Eliza was and what she was doing. And how the people at home were. What they were doing. Then he laughed. Of course he knew what they would be doing now. His people and all the other people would be sitting in front of the huge communal fire now. They would be talking and dancing. And others would be singing. The young ones would be playing and the old ones watching. Of course he knew what they would be doing now at home. . . .

But here it's so different. No one trusted anyone else. Leah said it was always fighting. Johannes was afraid of being sober. Daddy was never sober. Old Ma Plank sounded as though she was slightly crazy. And the thin one called Lena was one person when she was drunk, and another and very unhappy person when she was sober.

And Eliza, beautiful Eliza who could understand so much in one minute. She was also strange as soon as you looked at her again. He knew that he loved her and wanted her. But knowing that made him unhappy. Did not Leah say she wanted one who could read

52

books and dress like white men and speak their language? But Leah had also said she wanted him and he had to force her. And he would never force her. And this thing between them kept her from coming to him of her own free will. The ways of the city are truly strange, he decided as he stared at the Milky Way.

The old folk said that those who died became stars. He wondered if his mother was a star and whether she was up there and whether she could see him.

'Mother. Mother, are you there among the stars? And can you see me?'

He chuckled to himself. Fool! to be talking at the stars. It reminded him of his dog who always bayed at the moon. As if the moon cared!

Maisy came out and joined him.

'Are you still angry?'

He looked at her. Lines of good humour showed round her mouth and her laughing eyes were bright.

'No,' he said.

'You like her very much?'

'Like who?'

'I thought that's why you were angry.'

'I don't understand your talk.'

'It does not matter. . . . Leah tells me you are new to the city. How long have you been here?'

'I came four days ago.'

'Where from?'

Her voice was hoarse and rough but had an appealing warmth withal.

'From the north. Beyond Zoutpansberg. . . . And you?'

'I was born here.'

'In the city?' He looked curiously at her.

She laughed. He liked the sound of her hoarse laughter.

'Yes. In the city.'

'You've never been on the farms?'

'No.'

'Don't you long for the farms sometimes?'

'No. I have never been on a farm so I cannot long for it.'

'And you are not unhappy, like those others?' He jerked his head in the direction of those inside.

Maisy laughed. Her laughter rang out loud and hoarse and friendly. Two women and a man passing down the street, turned their heads and smiled. Maisy waved to them. They waved back.

'Who are they?' Xuma asked.

'I don't know.'

He looked at her. She was born here and she laughed when he asked her if she was unhappy.

She grabbed his arm and clung to it till the fits of laughter passed. Then she looked up into his face and wiped her tears.

'No, Xuma, I'm not unhappy. I don't like it. I like to be happy and to laugh. That is good. . . . I hear people dancing at the corner. Come, let's go too.'

'No.'

She tugged at his arms.

'Oh come on, Xuma,' she coaxed.

'No.'

She let go of his arm and faced him.

'You're waiting for her, heh?'

'Who?'

'You know who I mean. Eliza. But she won't have you. You're not good enough for *her*. She thinks she's a queen, that one! She wants people who smoke cigars like the white folk and have motor cars and wears suits every day. Come on, Xuma, don't waste your time on her, she'll just pull up her nose at you. I'll show you some fun! I'll show you the city can be good! Come. . . .'

'I'm tired. I began work at the mines today and I must rest.'

'We will drive the tiredness away, come!'

She dragged him off the verandah and up the street. The noise of people clapping hands and humming drew near. Maisy clung to his arm, shaking her hips and taking little fancy steps as they walked up the street. Every now and then she skipped away from him, swung around making her dress swish, bowed gracefully to him, then danced back and clung to his arm again. And the joy of living was so warm in her that it warmed him too. His eyes lighted up and he returned her smile.

On the corner of the street, under the light of the lamp, a group of men and women formed a ring. They clapped their hands and stamped their feet to a fast-moving rhythm and hummed. And one woman sang.

And in the centre of the ring a couple would dance and make signs to each other and speak in the language of movement. Then they would step back into the ring and two others would go forward into the centre of the ring. And they would speak with their hands and their feet and their hips and the glances of their eyes. And all the time the ring would call out words of praise and encouragement to them. And all the time one woman would sing words in a clear, beautiful voice and the others would hum and clap and stamp their feet, their faces alight with laughter and joy and their bodies swaying.

Xuma and Maisy joined the ring. And Xuma felt happy. And beside him Maisy, with shining eyes and flashing teeth, was clapping and swaying from side to side and encouraging him. He clapped and swayed and his teeth showed. Maisy nodded her approval.

A couple stepped into the ring. With commanding movements the man called the woman to him and told her to go on her knees in front of him. Disdainfully the woman danced away. Again the man commanded. The woman ignored him. He made to grab her. She danced away and evaded him.

The women in the ring applauded her, the men encouraged the man.

The man pulled himself up to his full height, and, trembling with anger, commanded the woman to go on her knees to him. Her eyes showed fear before his wrath, she cowered away and edged backward. The man stepped forward. The woman stepped back. Again he commanded and the trembling of his body was violent. But cowering fearfully, the woman still refused to go on her knees to him. He lashed out at her. She winced and staggered with pain, but still would not give in.

In desperation the man turned away.

The men in the ring expressed their sympathy. The women encouraged her to resist. And above it all was the clear voice of the woman singing.

Suddenly the man in the ring turns and dances up to the woman. He now pleads. He does not command any more. And pleading, he goes down on his knees. The woman dances a victory dance, full of triumph.

The women in the ring joined with her in her victory. The men share his humiliation with him.

Her victory dance stops suddenly. And lovingly she dances up to him, also pleading. She too goes down on her knees. They embrace each other. . . .

The couple stepped back. Another couple stepped into the centre of the ring. And so it went on.

Maisy nudged Xuma and indicated the centre of the ring. He laughed and nodded. They waited. As soon as the ring was clear they stepped forward. . . .

When it was over they went a little away from the ring and stood laughing. Xuma's face was wet with sweat. Maisy wiped his face with her handkerchief. They breathed heavily and leaned against each other.

'It is not good to be happy?' she asked.

'It is very good,' he said and looked into her laughing eyes. 'Let us join the ring again.'

'No,' she said and took his arm. 'It is late and you must rest. And I too must go to work in the morning.'

'Only for a little time, heh?'

'No! Xuma. At first you didn't want to come, now you don't want to leave. But we must, the others will be looking for you.'

'I am not a child.'

'Come on,' she said, and laughing, dragged him away.

Leah was on the verandah. She looked at Xuma.

'You have made the sour one laugh, Maisy.'

'It is easy. He wants someone to laugh and he will laugh too. Is it not so, Xuma?'

'This is a gay one,' he said and smiled.

'And my dancing?'

'This one wants you, Xuma,' Leah said dryly.

'And is that bad?' Maisy asked.

'Ask him,' Leah said.

'Or do you want him?' Maisy asked watching Leah carefully.

Leah tossed her head and laughed.

'Ask him that too.'

Maisy grinned and slipped her arm through Leah's. Leah patted her hand. Maisy's other arm was slipped through Xuma's arm.

'Eliza has come,' Leah said.

Xuma jerked his arm away but Maisy clung to it. Leah smiled.

56

'We will go in,' she said.

Eliza looked up as they entered. Beside her was a well-dressed, thin, unhealthy-looking young man.

Eliza looked from Xuma to Maisy and saw how Maisy leaned on Xuma.

'You look very happy, Maisy,' she said.

'I am, Eliza! I've just been dancing with Xuma. He dances very well, have you danced with him?'

'No.'

'And he's so strong. I like Xuma.'

Eliza stared at Maisy, and Maisy stared back at Eliza.

'Where is Johannes?' Xuma asked.

'He's sleeping,' Leah said.

'This is teacher Ndola,' Eliza said. 'I was out with him.'

'Did you have a good time?' Maisy asked.

'Yes.'

'We did too, didn't we, Xuma?'

'Oh yes, it was very good.'

'I'm tired,' Leah said, 'I want to go to sleep. Where will you sleep, Maisy, with Eliza or with Xuma?' There was a mocking dryness in Leah's voice.

Maisy ignored it.

'I will decide,' she said sweetly.

Leah's eyes hardened, then softened. She laughed.

'That tongue of yours, it will get you into trouble.'

'Good night,' Xuma said and went to the yard and to the back room.

He sat on the bed and held his head in his hands. Eliza had gone out with that sickly monkey dressed in the clothes of a white man. Why, even his hands were soft. But Maisy was good. Her he could understand. And for the first time since he had been in the city he had been happy. And she, Maisy, had done it. They had danced and it had been good. She was a good one, that one. And in her eyes there was an invitation. And she was kind too, she did not mock him. She helped him along with things he did not understand. And she felt soft and warm.

If she were with him now all the unhappiness would go, he knew that. Yet he longed for Eliza who was cold and had gone out with another man.

He blew out the candle and sat in the dark. He lit a cigarette.
There was a knock at the door.
'Yes?'
'Are you sleeping?'
It was Eliza's voice.
'No.'
'Can I come in?'
'Yes. Come in.'
She entered. He felt in his pockets till he found the box of matches.
'Do not make a light. I will open the window behind the bed and we can see by the light of the moon.'
She bumped into him, went round, and opened the window. The light of the moon streamed into the room. He could see the outline of Eliza near him.
'May I sit here?'
'Yes.'
There was silence broken by the noises that drifted in through the window from the outside world.
'How was the dancing?' Her voice was small.
'It was good.'
'Your face was happy when you came in and Maisy held your arm.'
'I was happy.'
'You like Maisy?'
'Yes. I can understand her and she's friendly and I was happy because she tried to make me happy.'
'Leah likes her too. She's always laughing and people like her.'
Again there was silence between them. Eliza fumbled in her pocket and found a cigarette.
'Give me a light.'
Xuma did.
'How did you find the mines?'
'It was all right.'
'What did you do?'
'I helped to start a mine-dump that would not grow.'
'Was it hard?'
'Yes, but not too hard.'
Eliza's cigarette glowed as she pulled at it. Then she sighed.

'Why did you come?' Xuma asked.

'Because I wanted to,' she said softly.

'You went out with your teacher.'

'You danced with Maisy.'

'Only because you were not here. ... Why did you come, to make a fool of me?'

'No. I came because I did not want to come and at the same time I wanted to come. Oh you don't understand!'

'What is it that I do not understand?'

'It's something inside me. Something hard that drives me. I don't know what it is. But one minute I'm like this and the next minute I'm different. One minute I know what I want, the next minute I do not know.'

'What do you want now?'

'I don't know! I came because I wanted to be with you, and now I'm here and I'm still not happy. But don't you understand?'

'Come here.' His voice was strong.

She moved closer to him. He put his arm round her and pressed her to his chest. Slowly the stiffness left her body till she lay softly against him. She sighed and nestled closer into the circle of his arm.

'You do not hate me?' she whispered.

'No.'

'You do like me, heh?'

'Yes.'

'Much?'

'Very much.'

'Maybe you love me?'

'Maybe. ... I don't know. ... You are like the devil in my blood.'

'I can laugh and dance just like Maisy, you wait. I will show you one day!'

She slipped her arms round his neck and clung to him.

'You are so strong. ... So big. ... It warms my blood, Xuma.'

She kissed him. A long warm, hard, passionate kiss. Xuma gathered her up and crushed her to him. She held him with all her strength.

Xuma's heart sang. She loved him! She loved him!

He bent her backward and leaned over her. Her eyes shone. And

59

as he looked into her shining eyes he saw a shadow creep into them. Her body stiffened. She pushed his hand away from her thigh and jumped away. He let her go.

'No!' she shouted. 'No!' She yelled it at the top of her voice. 'No! No!'

Then she flung herself on the bed and lay still.

Xuma struck a match and lit the candle. Eliza got up from the bed. She had her handkerchief between her teeth and tears were streaming down her face. But no sound came from her. She tried to speak but couldn't.

She went out.

For a long time Xuma sat staring into space. Then he blew out the candle and got into bed. But he could not sleep. He lay staring at the sky through the open window, and listened to the gradually fading noises till everything seemed to have gone to sleep and only the city hummed.

Then the door opened and Eliza came in again. She got into the bed beside him. He did not look at her.

'Xuma,' she said softly.

'Yes?'

'I am no good and I cannot help myself. It will be right if you hate me. You should beat me. But inside me there is something wrong. And it is because I want the things of the white people. I want to be like the white people and go where they go and do the things they do and I am black. I cannot help it. Inside I am not black and I do not want to be a black person. I want to be like they are, you understand, Xuma. It is no good but I cannot help it. It is just so. And it is that that makes me hurt you. ... Please understand.'

'How can I understand?'

Eliza sighed and went out again.

SIX

The warmth had gone out of the air, and slowly winter had come to Malay Camp, to Vrededorp, to Johannesburg. The days were cold now, and the nights were bitterly so. People wrapped themselves up warmly and snuggled closer to their fires. People slept close together to be warmer. Particularly in Malay Camp and Vrededorp.

Xuma had been in the city for three months now. He had left Leah's place over two months ago and lived in a room in Malay Camp. He had not been to see Leah since he left there. He did not want to go there for fear he should meet Eliza. And she was like a devil in his blood.

He could not forget her.

Leah he wanted to see; and the others too. Had they not been his first friends when he came to the city. Had they not given him food and a place to live. But because he feared seeing Eliza he would not go. So he had stayed away.

And this night, as he sat in the cold room with no fire, and there was no one to speak to, he longed for the warmth of Leah's place and for the brightness in Leah's eyes and for the drunken nonsense of Daddy and the wise, watching eyes of old Ma Plank, who saw everything and said nothing. He even longed to see the thin coloured woman, Lena, who was like a baby beside Johannes. He longed for them all and his heart felt heavy and the coldness in the room was great.

He lit his pipe and sucked it. Then he got up, put on his coat and went out. He shivered as the night air hit his face.

It was Saturday night and in spite of the cold the streets were crowded. But it was not as it had been that first Saturday when he had gone walking with Joseph. People moved slowly and clung to each other. And you could not make out the strong men. They were all dressed to keep out the cold. And there were no crowds standing on street corners talking. They all moved.

He went up the street and walked in the direction of the heart of Johannesburg. He passed a couple under a lamplight. The man had his arms round the woman. The woman was laughing into the man's face. He looked away and hurried past. And everywhere he saw couples. They walked close together to keep out the cold. And they all seemed so happy. Only he walked alone.

His shoes were thin and the cold came through. His toes began to ache. But it's not so bad, he thought, remembering all the clothes his white man had given him. And there were others who passed him who did not even have shoes. And many without coats and one could see it in their eyes, so it was not so bad. But even those whose eyes showed how cold they were were not alone. Most of them walked with a woman. Others had men friends. Only he walked alone.

He neared the heart of Johannesburg and the people grew fewer. There were more white people now and they were different. They did not walk or look like his people and it was as if they were not really there. He stepped aside for them to pass and he heard their voices, but they were strangers. He did not look at them or watch them carefully to see what they said and how their eyes looked and whether there was love in the eyes of the woman who hung on the arm of the man. They were not his people so he did not care.

He passed the window of a restaurant. Inside, white people sat eating and talking and smoking and laughing at each other. It looked warm and comfortable and inviting. He looked away quickly.

In another window there were cakes. He stopped and looked at them. He felt a tap on his shoulder and turned. It was a policeman. Without a word he fished his pass from his pocket and gave it to the policeman. The policeman looked at it, looked him up and down, and returned the pass to him. Xumas could see he was a kind one.

'Where are you going, Xuma?'

'I'm just walking.'

'Ah hah, why not go home and sit in front of the fire with your beer.'

Xuma smiled, 'You want me to go to jail?'

The policeman laughed, 'All right, but behave yourself.'

Xuma watched him go. Not a bad one that. Maybe he's new.

He carried on up the street and turned down Eloff Street. This was the heart of the city and the crowd was thick. It was difficult to move among all these white people, one had to keep on stepping aside and to watch out for the motor cars that shot past.

Xuma smiled bitterly. The only place where he was completely free was underground in the mines. There he was a master and knew his way. There he did not even fear his white man, for his white man depended on him. He was the boss boy. He gave the orders to the other mine boys. They would do for him what they would not do for his white man or any other white man. He knew that, he had found it out. And underground his white man respected him and asked him for his opinion before they did anything. It was so and he was at home and at ease underground.

His white man had even tried to make friends with him because the other mine boys respected him so much. But a white man and a black man cannot be friends. They work together. That's all. He smiled. He did not want the things of the white man. He did not want to be friends with the white man. Work for him, yes, but that's all. And didn't the others respect him more than they respected Johannes. It was because he did not say baas to the white man but knew how to deal with him.

Then he thought of Eliza again. And the pride vanished from his breast. He had tried to forget her but it was no good. Every day his longing for her grew more and more. But she wanted the things of the white man and for that reason he resented the white man.

'Look Di, there's Zuma!'

Xuma turned. It was his white man. And with him was a woman. And there was laughter in his eyes and a smile on his lips. It was the first time Xuma had seen Paddy laughing.

'Hello, Zuma!'

Paddy held out his hand. Xuma hesitated then shook it. Xuma smiled. The Red One had been drinking.

'This is my girl, Zuma. How is my taste?' Paddy laughed.

Xuma looked at the woman. She smiled at him and gave him her

hand. Passing white people stopped and turned. Xuma felt unhappy and wished the Red One would take his woman away. He
took the woman's hand. It was small and soft.

'So this is Zuma,' the woman said.

'It begins with an X, dear,' Paddy said.

'The Red One talks about you a lot, Zuma,' she said.

'We are blocking traffic,' Paddy said and took Xuma's arm.

Paddy led him a little way down the street and turned off into a
little alley.

'I live here,' Paddy told him.

'Bring him up, Red,' the woman said.

'Good idea!' Paddy exclaimed. 'Come, Zuma, you will eat with
us?'

'No,' Xuma said.

'Come on!' Paddy insisted and half pushed him into the lift.

They got out and the woman led the way into the flat.

'This is my home,' Paddy said.

Xuma looked around. He had never seen a place like that
before.

There was no fire, but it was warm.

'Sit down, Zuma,' the woman said.

Xuma sat on the edge of the chair. The woman took off her coat
and went into another room. Paddy stretched himself on a settee
and smiled at Xuma.

The woman came in with three glasses.

'This will warm you,' she said, giving Xuma one.

Paddy raised his glass.

'To the best mine boy, Zuma!'

'To Zuma,' the woman said and smiled at him.

Paddy and Di emptied their glasses. Xuma sat holding his. He
could still feel the woman's hand in his. It was so small and soft.
And she was very good to look at but he didn't want to look at
her.

'Drink yours, Zuma,' she said.

The wine warmed Xuma. She took the empty glass from him
and turned on the radio.

'Everything is ready,' she said to Paddy. 'Put it on the trolley and
bring it in.'

Paddy went out.

64

Xuma thought: now I understand what Eliza wants. But these things are only for white people. It is foolish to think we can get them.

He looked round the room. Yes, it was fine. Carpets on the floor, books, radio. Beautiful things everywhere. Fine, all fine, but all the white man's things. And all foolishness to want the white man's things. To drink wine and keep the bottle on the table without fear of the police, how could a black person do it. And how could Eliza be like this white woman of the Red One.

Di followed his gaze round the room.

'Do you like it?'

'Heh?' He looked startled.

'I mean the room,' she said.

'It is fine,' he said and looked at her.

Her eyes looked kindly at him and dimples appeared on her cheeks when she smiled. Just like Eliza's dimples. And it seemed that her eyes understood what he was thinking. He looked away from her.

'The Red One wants you to be his friend,' she said.

Again Xuma looked at her. And again it seemed that she understood everything that went on in his mind. And as he watched her a smile slowly broke over her face.

'He is white,' Xuma said.

The smile faded from her face and there was sadness in her eyes.

And suddenly Xuma felt sorry for her and was surprised at himself for feeling sorry for a white person. And there was no reason for it either.

'And so you cannot be friends,' she said, and in her eyes was the same look he had seen many times in the eyes of the Red One.

Paddy came in with the food. Xuma felt ill at ease. But Paddy and Di talked and did not notice him, and soon he forgot his discomfort and ate.

When they had finished eating they drank more wine. And Xuma and Paddy talked about the mines and the funny things that happened there and soon they were all laughing. And in spots Xuma forgot that they were white and even spoke to the woman. Then Paddy took the things away.

Xuma looked at the woman and suddenly wanted to tell her

about Eliza. But he didn't know how to begin. She gave him a cigarette and smoked one herself. Eliza smoked too. Xuma looked at Di and smiled.

'What are you smiling at?'

'My girl smokes too.'

'What's wrong with that?'

Xuma was silent.

'What is she called?'

'Eliza.' He wanted to tell her then, but the words would not come.

'Tell me,' Di said.

'What?'

'What you want to tell me. The Red One will be back soon and I know you don't want him to hear.'

'You know everything.'

'No. But I know this. Tell me.'

Xuma stared at her. She met his stare and smiled.

'You are a good one,' he said.

'Thank you. I'm your friend. Tell me.'

'She's a teacher and she wants to be like white people. She wants a place like this place and clothes like yours and she wants to do the things you do. It is all foolishness for she is not white. But she cannot help herself and it makes her unhappy sometimes.'

'And you?'

'It makes me unhappy too, for she wants me and she does not want me. But it is foolishness.'

'It is not foolishness, Zuma.'

'She cannot have your things.'

'But is not the heart the same, Zuma?'

'No. I care only for my people.'

'No, Zuma.'

'But it is so and where is the good in wishing.'

'Listen, Zuma. I am white and your girl is black, but inside we are the same. She wants the things I want and I want the things she wants. Eliza and I are the same inside, truly, Zuma.'

'But it cannot be.'

'It is so, Zuma, we are the same inside. A black girl and a white girl, but the same inside.'

'The same?'

'The same.'

'But it is wrong.'

'It is right, Zuma, I know.'

'No!'

'Yes!'

'It cannot be. You are good, but it cannot be.'

'It is. You do not believe me but it is so. . . .'

Paddy came in. Xuma looked at Di then got up.

'I must go,' he said.

'Not yet, Zuma,' Paddy said, 'it is early still.'

'All right, Zuma,' Di said.

Paddy looked at Di then at Xuma and smiled.

'Do you like my woman?'

Xuma smiled. 'She's a good one, and you are lucky, Red One.'

'I will take you down,' Paddy said.

Di took Xuma's hand and smiled into his eyes.

'I am right.'

'Maybe. But I don't think so.'

He followed Paddy to the lift.

Paddy returned and slowly shut the door behind him. Di watched him. He went to the settee and pulled her down beside him. He slipped his arm round her shoulder and they sat like that for a while.

'What do you think of him,' he asked finally.

'What is there to think? . . . He's just a mine boy.'

'He's a grand fellow.'

'Yes. Grand, but not a human being yet. Just a mine boy. His girl's human and he can't understand her. He can't understand her wanting the things I want and have. And another thing you're wrong about – he does not dislike you, you're just not of the same world, Red.'

'That's nonsense, Di.'

'Think it out for yourself.'

'That fellow's as human as I am.'

'No, Red, he accepts what you wouldn't. That's part of the reason why he's so popular among all the other whites. He's all right. You can't say the same about Chris's boy.'

'I think you are wrong, Di.'

She smiled bitterly and looked at him.

'Yes, I know, Red. A man's a man for a' that. A man's a man to the extent that he asserts himself. There's no assertion in your mine boy. There is confusion and bewilderment and acceptance. Nothing more. Oh, he's human all right; he talks, he eats, he feels, he thinks, he gets lonely; but that's all.'

'He has dignity and pride.'

'So has an animal, Red. You've got this all wrong. The man in your Zuma has not come out yet, so he looks beautiful and strong and perfect and has dignity, so you say that is your future native. That is not true.'

Paddy looked at her. His face clouded. They were silent for a very long time. Di got up and went into the kitchen.

'You make it very difficult, Di,' Paddy called out. 'You make it sound as though there's no hope anywhere.'

Di laughed and her voice was sweet.

'Never again will I take up with an Irishman,' she said. 'One moment you are at one extreme and the next you are at the other.'

'Be serious, Di.'

There was a pause from the kitchen. He waited. Then her voice came to him. It was slow and hesitant and yet very-matter-of-fact.

'So many of the people who consider themselves progressive have their own weird notions about the native, but they all have one thing in common. They want to decide who the good native is and they want to do good things for him. You know what I mean. They want to lead him. To tell him what to do. They want to think for him and he must accept their thoughts. And they like him to depend on them. Your Zuma makes an excellent "good native" for progressive folk. That's why you like him.'

'That's not true, Di. And I think you're being unfair.'

'I'm sorry, Red, but I honestly believe that.'

'In any case your little theory holds no water with Zuma. He is unfriendly towards me.'

'Yes, that's the one snag, but it doesn't prove anything. And beside, he's not being unfriendly towards you; you two just belong to different worlds. But the whole point is that a native who wants the things the whites have is suspect if he does not apply to them for leadership.'

68

Di came back into the room and they sat facing each other.

'So?'

'So nothing.'

'That leaves a pretty hopeless position for your hypothetical progressives.'

'Yes, until they accept the fact that the natives can lead; not only themselves but the whites as well.'

'And what about Zuma?'

'I am more interested in his girl. She wants and she resents. She's a social animal; he's not.'

'You're wrong, Di. That girl is tragedy already. For Zuma there's still hope. You're translating your wishes into facts. Merely to want and resent is not enough.'

'But it's human.'

'Yes, darling, it's human. But even that is not enough. You can sneer as hard as you like but Zuma is strong and strength is important. The thing you miss is that he's as human as his girl or I or you, and that very humanness will wake him up. Sneer as much as you like against your progressives, Di, but for God's sake have faith in human beings. It is not enough to destroy, you must build as well. Build up a stock of faith in your breast in native Zuma, mine boy, who has no social conscience, who cannot read or write and cannot understand his girl wanting what you want.

'I'll tell you something, my dear. The first day he came to the mines Smid told him to push a truck and he didn't know anything about it. . . .'

Xuma was glad to be away from the two white people. It had been uncomfortable in there. And the more they had tried to make him feel at ease the more difficult it had been. Only with the woman had it not been so bad. She had great understanding, that one, great wisdom. And he had seen the Red One smile for once.

Only when he was alone with the woman had he felt all right. He wondered what made him tell her about Eliza. Maybe it was because she understood and was so wise. But she could not be very wise. Did she not say it was a good thing for Eliza to want the things of the white people? And that was foolishness, for Eliza could never get those things.

But they were good things. He had seen them with his own eyes.

And now he understood how it was that Eliza wanted them. Now he knew what it was she wanted. And knowing made things less difficult in his breast.

He crossed the street and wended his way back to Malay Camp. The cold was not so bad now. The food they had given him had been good, but not solid. No mealie meal in it. And food without mealie meal or lots of bread could not fill a man properly. He smiled. They had been kind. They had meant well. And the Red One was lucky to have such a woman who was friendly even to a black person.

For she was friendly in a different way from the Red One. With the Red One one felt that he wanted you to trust him and go to him when there was trouble. And it was hard to be friendly with a white person thus. With the woman it was different. When she asked about one's thoughts there was nothing behind her brain. So he could talk to her.

Gradually he left the heart of the city behind him. The white people thinned out. And more and more he saw only his people. And more and more the feeling of watchfulness and alertness to step out of the way left him.

Now he rubbed against people and did not step out of the way. He bumped against them and felt their warmth and softness. It was all right here. This was Malay Camp. And the few white people here were Syrians who sold wine to the black people and coloured people. Why, some of their women even did business sleeping with black men. They were all right.

He turned down Jeppe Street. Lower down the street a crowd of people stood. They were looking upward. He hurried down. When he got to the people he stopped and looked up. There was nothing to see.

'What is it?' he asked and a man beside him.

'I don't know,' the man said.

Xuma edged away, still looking at the rooftops. He bumped into a woman.

'What is it?'

'There is a man up there,' the woman said, 'and the police are chasing him.'

'Where?'

The woman pointed. He looked closely. Yes, there he was! He

70

was crawling along a slanting roof, and close behind him was a policeman. Xuma held his breath. The roof sloped steeply. One wrong move and the man would plunge down, either to death or a broken body. And for the policeman it was the same too.

A yell of fear rose from the crowd. The man had lost his hold and was slowly sliding down the sloping roof. Down he came. Down. Down. Now he was at the edge of the roof. If he could not stop himself he would plunge to the ground. One leg came over the side of the roof. Then the other. He was going to fall.

Xuma held his breath. His heart pounded furiously.

The man got hold of the edge of the roof with his hands and swung there. A tremble of fear passed through the crowd. The policeman edged nearer.

There was a bustle in the crowd and a slender, well-dressed man pushed his way to the fore. He was dressed in the clothes of the white people and behaved like the white people. He pushed people out of the way. Unwillingly the people shifted their gaze from the man swinging on the side of the roof and looked at the man. 'Who is he?' they asked one another. 'And what does he think he is?' yet others asked.

And someone whispered to his neighbour, 'That is the doctor. Doctor Mini.' And the whisper was carried along and passed round the crowd. Xuma looked at the doctor.

The doctor stared up at the swinging man.

'Who is he?'

No one answered the doctor.

Again the doctor spoke in his sharp, thin voice:

'What has he done? Did any one see?'

'He was playing dice,' a ragged man said sullenly.

A woman cried out. The policeman who was edging nearer had been joined by another. Both were edging nearer. Carefully and slowly. But it was not that that had made the woman cry out. She had seen one of the man's hands slip. He was now holding on by one hand only. The crowd was tense. This was the kill. Automatically they moved forward in a body. The doctor was in the lead. Xuma pushed forward.

Then the man up there, hanging between the sky and the earth, let go his grip as though he were tired. There was a uniform sigh from the crowd. For a minute the man was in space. Then with a dull thud he was on the ground. For a minute he lay where he had dropped. The crowd was rooted to where it stood.

Then the man moved. The crowd became individuals again. The doctor ran forward and knelt beside the man. The crowd pressed close around.

'Give him air,' the doctor said.

Xuma pushed the crowd back, 'Give him air,' he repeated.

The doctor felt the man's body all over.

'It's all right, only his arm is broken.'

The doctor looked at Xuma.

'Help me get away,' the man whispered.

Suddenly the crowd parted and moved back. Policemen pushed through.

'Stand back,' the foremost shouted.

Xuma moved back with the crowd. Only the doctor remained.

'You!' the policeman said to the doctor. 'Didn't you hear?'

The doctor got up and looked at the policeman.

'I'm Doctor Mini.'

The policeman laughed. Another behind him pushed forward and smacked the doctor in the face. Xuma bunched his fist and took a deep breath.

'You'll hear about this,' the doctor said.

The second policeman again raised his hand.

'You'd better not,' another policeman said and stepped forward. 'He is a doctor.'

The other two looked at the older policeman. There was disbelief in their eyes.

'It's true,' the older policeman said.

'I want to take this man with me,' the doctor said, looking at the older policeman. 'His arm is badly broken and he's got to be looked after.'

'No bloody fear,' the first policeman said. 'He's going where he belongs, in jail.'

The doctor took out a card and gave it to the older policeman. 'I'm attached to the General Hospital, and this is my home address if you want me. I'm taking this man with me. You can come and get him in an hour's time. And when you come I want to lodge a charge against this man for assaulting me.'

The policemen looked at each other nonplussed. There was an

72

obstinate look in the eyes of the first. Fear was showing in the eyes of the second. The older man looked tired and weary. He took the card from the doctor's hand and nodded. The first one opened his mouth. The second one shook his head. The first one kept silent.

'Will someone help me carry him to my car?' the doctor said.

The first policeman swung round and looked at the crowd. There was a threat in his eyes. He held his club menacingly. The crowd remained where it was.

The doctor tried to lift the man but could not.

Xuma took a deep breath, bunched his fists, and stepped forward. The policeman tightened his grip on his club and waved it from side to side. He stared hard at Xuma. Xuma returned the stare and kept going forward. He pushed past the policemen. The doctor looked up and smiled.

'Lift him but be careful of that arm.'

'Just a minute,' the first policeman said and prodded Xuma with his club.

Xuma got up. His body trembled. His fists were bunched into hard balls.

'Where's your pass? Let me see it.'

Xuma took out his pass and gave it to the policeman. The policeman looked at it for a long time then returned it.

Xuma picked up the wounded man. The crowd made a passage. The doctor led the way through. Xuma followed him. The doctor opened the door of his car and helped Xuma to ease the man gently on to the back seat.

'Can you come with me to help me carry him in?'

Xuma nodded.

'Get in there beside him and hold him so that his arm does not bump against anything.'

The doctor shut the door then got into the front and started the car. Before the car moved off the doctor turned his eyes and looked to where the crowd had been. Xuma looked too. The crowd was scattering in all directions. The two policemen were chasing them. Only the older one stood where they had left him. Stood with that weary look on his face.

The car moved off, slowly and carefully.

The doctor took out a cigarette and handed the packet to Xuma.

'What's your name?'
'Xuma.'
'Been in the city long?'
'Three months.'
'I see.'

For the rest of the way they drove in silence. Xuma kept looking from the man by his side to the man in front. They were both his people but they were so different. For the one by his side he didn't have much respect. There were so many like him. They drank and they fought and they gambled. And there were so many like that in the city. He had watched them. He knew them. But this other one was different. Different from all the other people who had stood around there. Even the white people saw the difference and treated him differently. No one Xuma knew could have done what this one had done. And yet this one was one of his people.

At the other end of Malay Camp the doctor pulled up. Between them they carried the man into a house.

A coloured woman who was almost white and who was dressed like the white people, met them at the door. And inside the house was even more beautiful than the place of the Red One. There were all the things he had seen in the Red One's place and even more.

They carried the man into the surgery. The woman helped the doctor to take off his coat and gave him a thin, white one.

Quickly, deftly, carefully the doctor worked on the man's arm. And all the while the woman was there, giving him things and helping him and talking to him. Xuma sat on a little chair and watched.

Maybe the woman is his wife, Xuma thought.

And when they had finished bandaging the man and the doctor had washed his hands and the woman kissed him, Xuma knew she was his wife.

'There!' the doctor said and smiled at Xuma.

The woman smiled too. Maybe I should go now, Xuma thought.

Another woman, a black one, came into the room with a glass. She made the wounded one drink out of it. The wounded one sat up.

'Thank you, Doctor,' he said. 'Maybe I can go now.'

'No, not yet. I told the police to come in an hour. I don't think they will come, but it's best to wait and see. You lie down and get some of your strength back.'

'But they will arrest me.'

'If they do I will charge the policeman who assaulted me. But if I let you go I'll get into trouble.'

The wounded man looked round the room but said nothing.

'Perhaps you will wait too, Xuma, then you can be my witness. You saw everything.'

Xuma nodded.

The coloured woman put a blanket over the wounded man.

'Come, Xuma, we will have some tea,' the doctor said.

They went out and left only the wounded one behind. In the other room there was a big fire. And there was a radio too, and light that one put on by pressing a little thing in the wall. No oil lamp and candles. Xuma looked round the room. The doctor followed his gaze and smiled. Xuma looked at him and saw the smile. He felt as he had felt in the place of the Red One. As though he did not belong there and it was wrong for him to be there.

The doctor saw the shadow pass over his face.

'What is it?'

'This is like the white people's place.'

The doctor and his wife laughed.

'No, Xuma,' the doctor said. 'Not like the white people's place. Just a comfortable place. You are not copying the white man when you live in a place like this. This is the sort of place a man should live in because it is good for him. Whether he is white or black does not matter. A place like this is good for him. It is the other places that are the white people's. The places they make you live in.'

'Doctor! Doctor!'

The black woman came into the room. There was distress and agitation on her face.

'What is it, Emily?'

'The one you were bandaging has gone, Doctor. He has gone out through the window.'

'Oh. . . .'

Xuma watched the doctor's face. For a minute there was sadness and hopelessness in it. Like the faces of the men who had worked on the pile of fine, wet, white sand that would not grow less. It was there for a minute, then it was gone, and his face was again cold and calm and hard to make out.

The doctor got up and went to the surgery. The others followed him. The blanket was on the floor. The window was open. A cool breeze blew in. The man had gone.

The coloured woman took the doctor's arm. Emily went and shut the window.

'You can go now, Xuma,' the doctor said harshly without looking at him.

Xuma felt hurt. He had done nothing. He had stayed because the doctor had asked him, and now, because the other man had gone, the doctor spoke to him in a hard voice. He was angry, but more than the anger he felt the hurt.

He turned abruptly and walked to the door. The doctor's wife followed him. She held out her hand and smiled at him.

'Thank you very much,' she said.

Xuma took her hand. It was soft and small like the white woman's.

SEVEN

It was getting late but Xuma did not want to go back to his room yet. There was nothing to do there. Only to sit down in the cold. Or get into a cold bed. And that was no good either. He knew he would not sleep and he did not want to lie awake in a cold bed. He walked away from the doctor's house. He looked up. The sky seemed very far and it was very hard to see the stars. He saw one for a second and then it was gone again.

He turned a corner and suddenly became aware of Malay Camp. Became aware of it as he had not been before.

Malay Camp. A row of streets crossing another row of streets. Mostly narrow streets. Mostly dirty streets. Mostly dark streets. A row of houses crossing another row of houses. And so it went on. Streets crossing streets. Houses crossing houses.

Leaning, dark houses that hid life and death and love and hate and would not show anything to the passing stranger. Puddles of dirty muddy water on the sandy pavements. Little children playing in these puddles. Groups of men gambling on street corners. Groups of children walking down the streets carefully studying the gutters and vying with each other to pounce upon dirty edibles, and fighting each other for them. Prostitutes on street corners and pimps calling after them.

And from somewhere, the low monotonous wail of a broken-down piano thumping out an unchanging rhythm, and the sound of thudding feet dancing to it. Shouts and screams and curses. Fighting and thieving and lying.

But above it all, the real Malay Camp. The warmth in the air even on a cold night. The warmth of living bodies; of living, breathing, moving people. A warmth that was richer than the air and the earth and the sun. Richer than all things. The warmth of life, throbbing. Of hearts pounding. Of silence and of sound. Of movement and of lack of movement. A warm, thick, dark blanket of life. That was Malay Camp. Something nameless and living. A stream of dark life.

Xuma tried to think clearly and to arrange his thoughts in word-patterns, but failed. When he looked at the streets and houses and people, they were just streets and houses and people. The feeling that had passed over him was like a dream, unreal.

'I will go to Leah's place,' he said to himself and turned his steps in that direction.

It was Saturday night and he expected a crowd at Leah's place. But it was silent when he got there, and the yard gate was shut on the inside. He went to the front door and knocked. He waited then knocked again.

He remembered that first night he had come to this place. It seemed so long ago now. It was hard to believe it. So many things had happened since. He could not even remember what he looked like then. He knocked again. Louder.

The door opened and old Ma Plank looked out at him. It took some time for her to recognize him. Then she burst out laughing her cackling laugh and pulled him in.

'Xuma! Where have you been all this time. We have talked and talked and talked about you. Come in! Come in!'

It was like coming home. Here was old Ma Plank. The same as ever. The same wise devils in her eyes that told you that though she did not talk much she understood much.

'It is very silent tonight,' he said.

'The police are around. Many women have been arrested selling.'

'And Leah knew?'

'Leah pays to know.'

'Did she warn them?'

Ma Plank cocked her eyebrows at him and laughed with derision.

'You are still a fool.'

The house, too, was silent. Like it had been that first morning when he had woken in it. He followed Ma Plank into the kitchen. There was a fire. And near it, on the floor, Daddy was deep in a

78

drunken sleep. His mouth was wide open and a stream of saliva trickled down the side of his face.

'Where are the others?'

'They went to the Bioscope. Leah, Eliza and Maisy. Joseph they caught two weeks ago. He's in for six months. No fine.'

'Maisy's with them?'

'Didn't you hear me?' Ma Plank looked sideways at him.

'You lie, old woman!'

She laughed and he joined her.

'I said nothing.'

'Not with your tongue, but with your eyes, and you lied.'

'Ah! And what did I lie about?'

'You think there's something between Maisy and me.'

'So . . .?'

'Yes. And it's no good sitting there saying so and trying to be like an ostrich! An ostrich has feathers and you're an old woman!'

Ma Plank's sides shook as she cackled with laughter. Xuma tried to keep a straight face and to look severely at her. But this was like home and it was hard not to join in the merry laughter of the old woman.

When the shaking of her sides had stopped and she had wiped the tears from her eyes she patted his arm and there was softness on her lined and leathery old face.

'So the city has taught you to speak, heh? That's good. You were very silent when you first came. And it is not good for a man to be silent. . . . Tell me, have you eaten?'

'Yes. I met my white man and he took me to his place to eat.'

'Ahah! . . . A proper gentleman now, heh? He eats with the white people. . . . And look at his clothes! No wonder he left us!'

Her eyes twinkled.

'You are a foolish old woman!' Xuma said and looked at his clothes. He looked at the fire. 'Tell me about Eliza.'

'You still think of her?' the old woman's voice was soft.

'Yes.'

'She's still the same. Sometimes she cries. Sometimes she fights. Sometimes she will not speak to anyone. And then again sometimes she's all right.'

'And that teacher man?'

'I don't know which you mean. There are so many. They come and she gets tired of them and they don't come any more.'

'I see.'

'And you?'

'I work. . . . That's all.'

'We thought maybe you had a woman.'

'No.'

'Johannes tells us they like you at the mines.'

'Does she go out much?'

'Sometimes, and sometimes she stays in all the time. I know what you fear but I think you are wrong. She's not a loose one. Maybe one man, and then again maybe no man knows her. Once there was a man but he went away. It was a long time ago.'

'How do you know?'

'Because I have eyes and I am not jealous like you. You all say "Old woman" but I can see things.'

Xuma stared into the fire. On the floor Daddy grunted and kicked in his sleep. Swear words tumbled out of his mouth.

Daddy rolled on to his side and began to piddle. A pool of water grew on the floor. Xuma watched it, disgust written all over his face.

Daddy grunted again then rolled into the pool he had made.

'You scorn him, heh, Xuma?'

Xuma was startled by Ma Plank's voice.

'He's a man, and see what he does.'

'I have seen, Xuma. And I have seen even worse.' She sighed.

Xuma kept his eyes on the fire.

'You scorn him, heh? Yet when he first came to the city he was a man. Such a man! He was strong and he was feared and he was respected. And now you scorn him. You may think I am an old woman but I tell you, Xuma, he was a man such as I have never seen.'

Ma Plank smiled thoughtfully and looked into the fire, and when she spoke again her voice was tinged with bitterness:

'When he walked down the street women stopped and looked at him and men greeted him. Everyone respected his wisdom. And they came to him when they were in trouble and he helped them. Even the white ones respected him. And now you scorn him.

'He had money then, and many friends. Men thought it an

honour to be his friend and women longed for him. And when there was trouble about the passes he stood at the head of the people and he spoke to hundreds of them and the police feared him.

'He understood too much and it made him unhappy and he became like Eliza. Only he fought. And listen, Xuma, that one lying there in his own piss is wiser than Eliza. He can read and write even better than she can. He found Leah in the street and looked after her.

'Yes, Xuma, you scorn him. But I tell you he was a man such as I have never seen. . . .'

Xuma looked at Ma Plank. Her eyes were wet. And tears ran unheeded down her face. But there was a strange light in them. It was as though she could still see the man all men respected.

Xuma looked at Daddy. His clothes had absorbed the pool he had made. Xuma wanted to say something but there was nothing to say. Ma Plank looked at him through her tears. He patted her hand awkwardly and stared at a corner of the room. Ma Plank got up.

'I will make some tea,' she said.

Xuma looked at Daddy sleeping a drunken sleep in his piddle and tried to see him as a sober man, respected and followed by the other people. But how could he? He had never seen Daddy sober. He had never seen Daddy stand upright without swaying from one side to the other. And yet Ma Plank had said he was a man such as she had never seen. And it was true, for in her voice had been the ring of truth and in her eyes the light of truth. And now he was there, on the floor, soaked in his own piddle. But how could it be?

'The others have come back, I can hear them,' Ma Plank said.

Xuma listened to the footsteps. They were drawing near. Would Eliza be pleased to see him? What would Leah say? And the other one, would there still be laughter in her eyes? The door opened. He looked up.

Leah came in first. Her eyebrow lifted and the side of her mouth smiled when she saw him. That was all. Then came Eliza. She looked at him and there was a strange light in her eyes, then she looked away. And then came Maisy with the laughter in her eyes. And when she saw him the laughter spread to her face. She was the only one who greeted him.

Xuma felt dissatisfied. Leah and Eliza behaved as though he had been there all the time. It was too ordinary. He choked down the joy of greeting that was in his heart.

Leah went and stood over Daddy, then she bent and picked him up as one would pick up a child and carried him out of the room. Easily, with the strength of the strong.

Eliza took off her coat and undid the kerchief round her head. Then she sat down and held her hands to the fire. Xuma looked at her hands. They were soft. He felt their softness without touching them. Like the hands of the white woman, and the hands of the doctor's wife.

He looked at her arms and shoulders, at the rising and falling of her bosom, at the curve where her neck joined her face, at the smooth softness of her face, the darkness of her eyes, and desire was strong in him.

Ma Plank made the tea and gave them each a mug.

And in the room there were only the two of them. The others did not matter. They were not really there. Only he and Eliza.

Under the sharpness of his stare she raised her eyes and looked at him. And around them was darkness. He could only see the shadow of her face and the brightness of her eyes. And for her, too, it was so. All else faded. Only the two of them, there. Alone in the world. Alone everywhere. . . .

Maisy looked from Xuma to Eliza, then at Ma Plank. With a slight movement Ma Plank shook her head. Maisy looked away.

Leah returned.

'Well,' she said, looking at Xuma.

And again they were all there, Ma Plank and Maisy and the fire and room and the window and the sound of the street, and above them all was Leah. Xuma looked up at her.

'How are you?' Leah asked.

Xuma smiled. 'As always,' he replied.

Ma Plank gave Leah a mug of tea.

'It is a long time,' Leah said and looked from him to Eliza.

She understands everything, Xuma thought, just as always.

'It is the same,' he said.

She nodded and stared into the fire. Then she looked up and focused her eyes on Maisy.

'This one has longed for you.'

Xuma looked at Maisy. There was no laughter in her eyes as she looked him straight in the face. Leah laughed softly. A flush darkened the pale yellow of Maisy's skin. She lowered her eyes. When she looked up again the laughter was back in her eyes. And the flush and the laughter were to her very becoming, and Xuma saw her comeliness. It showed in his eyes for a brief spell.

Eliza looked from Xuma to Maisy, and then at Leah. And suddenly she got up and left the room. Again Leah laughed softly.

'She is still the same but she has not forgotten you; and you?' There was mockery in Leah's voice. It was harsh and brittle.

Ma Plank looked sharply at Leah. Maisy made a nervous movement with her head and laughed. Her laughter rang false. Xuma looked at Leah. Her eyes were hard and brooding and they were focused on the red glow of the fire.

'I met a boy from the mines and asked him about you,' Maisy said tentatively.

'Yes,' Xuma said without interest.

'But he was not from your mine,' Maisy said.

'Leah!' Xuma said.

Leah looked up. His voice had been hard and firm. It had shaken her.

'Yes?'

'Do you want me to go?'

'Yes!'

Xuma got up.

'But Leah. . . .' Ma Plank and Maisy said together.

'Shut up!' Leah said.

'Good night,' Xuma said and went out.

Maisy got up and hurried to the door.

'Come back!' Leah shouted.

Maisy hesitated, then came back to her seat.

Leah watched Maisy. And the crooked smile was back on the side of her face and her eyes were hard and brooding. Then, suddenly, she went out.

Maisy wanted to follow her but Ma Plank motioned her back to her seat.

Leah hurried down the street after Xuma. She caught up with him at the corner.

'Xuma!' she called.

He stopped and waited. He did not turn round. She was close behind him now. She stopped and looked at his back.

'Xuma.'

'Yes?'

There was a long pause. He knew she wanted him to turn round but he could not. He did not know whether he wanted to or not. He just could not.

'Xuma.' Her voice was soft and pleading.

His heart jumped with joy. Leah's voice was soft and pleading. Soft and pleading. Soft and pleading. . . .

He turned. She was close to him and there were tears in her eyes and her hands worked. An unknown tide of warmth shot through his body. She smiled through her tears.

Then, quickly, she grabbed him and clung to him, her head on his chest, her body shaking with sobs. He put his arms round her and held her tight.

Passing strangers looked at them.

And then, as quickly as she had grabbed him, Leah pushed him away. Again she was hard and strong. She brushed the tears from her eyes and smiled.

'There is a devil in me tonight,' she said. 'Come. We will walk for a little before we return to the house, heh?'

They turned the corner and walked in silence. Around them were people. People moving up and down. Some slowly, some hurrying. And around them and around the people, and above them all, was the din of the city.

The rumble of trams and trains, the noise of cars, the voices of people, the tramp of feet, all these created a din that was at once divorced from its causes and had an individuality all its own.

A clear, distinctive hum, throbbing from the bowels of the earth, from the mouths and hearts of men, from the machines, and rising. Rising high above its causes.

They passed a crooked lamp-post. A young man and his girl were locked in warm embrace.

'They arrested Joseph,' Leah said. 'I think there is someone who is betraying me and I cannot find out who it is. The police know what I do and when I do it. I can feel it.'

She looked at him then looked away.

'Are you angry with me?' he asked.

84

She laughed. 'You are a simple one, Xuma. You are a fool with people.'

Xuma smiled. There was a strange peacefulness in his heart. He liked it when she said he was a fool with people. He did not think it was true but he liked it. And it was so good to walk here with her. It was like being at home in the country again. Just walking quietly. Thus had he walked with his mother. And thus his mother had rebuked him.

And there was a gentleness in the air of Malay Camp. Perhaps it had been there all the time, but he only noticed it now.

It was like that first night when he had met Leah. They did not say much but they understood. She had known he was all right just by looking at him. So it is with people in the country. They understand and they know. And now it was like that again.

'You are a good one,' he said and took her arm.

She let him hold her arm for a little while then pulled it away.

'We must go back,' she said and the softness had gone out of her voice. It was impersonal again, matter-of-fact.

When they got back Eliza had returned to the kitchen and sat reading in front of the fire. She did not look up when they entered. Only Ma Plank and Maisy did. The laughter had gone out of Maisy's eyes, but it was there, peeping out behind the shadows, ready to burst forth again. Ma Plank was the same as always. She saw everything and said nothing.

'You will sleep here,' Leah said to Xuma. 'Come now, it is late.'

'Where will he sleep?' Ma Plank asked.

'In the little room. Maisy can sleep with me and Eliza can sleep in her room.'

'I will read for you,' Eliza said, looking at Xuma.

'It is late,' Leah said with her eyes on Eliza.

'Good night,' Maisy said and went out.

'Let her read,' Ma Plank said and went to the door.

Leah shrugged. The left side of her mouth creased. She followed Ma Plank. The candle flickered as the door shut behind them.

Eliza looked up at him and smiled.

'Shall I read?'

'Yes.'

She opened the book and read. It was the story of the Zulu wars.

And Zulu is a beautiful and colourful language and Eliza's voice was soft and the words kept coming till Xuma was caught up in the spell. And again the impis were ready to charge the white man who would steal their lands. And many died, but many more came forward to fight. But in the end they were beaten and the land taken from them for the white man was stronger. And the sorrow in Xuma's heart was great because they had lost the fight and it showed in his eyes.

Eliza closed the book.

'It is good,' he said, 'but it is sad that we lost.'

'Yes.'

The candle had burned itself out. It gave a last flicker and died. They sat in the glow of the firelight. Eliza leaned forward and lit a cigarette from the fire. It reminded him of the white woman of the Red One.

'I have seen the things of the white man,' he said.

'Yes.' There was no interest in her voice.

'I will go and sleep now,' he said.

She looked at him but said nothing. He went out into the yard and down to the room at the far end.

The room was just as it had been when he had left it. Nothing had been changed. He undressed and got into bed and blew out the candle.

It had been like home when only Ma Plank and Daddy had been there. But when the others came it was different. Not as it had been before he had left. Even Leah had changed.

The door opened and Eliza came in. Her teeth chattered. He felt a tight band round his heart. He remembered that other night.

'Leave me,' he said.

'No.'

He turned his head away from her. She got into the bed. She was cold. He could feel it. Her body shivered. She touched his hand but he pulled it away.

She relaxed. Her teeth stopped chattering. Her body stopped shivering. She lay quite still, not trying to touch him and not moving away.

Xuma felt the madness of desire rising in him. It would kill him soon.

'Leave me,' he repeated.

She rolled on her side and pressed against him, forcing him to feel the nearness of her.

'I love you,' she said.

Xuma crushed her soft, warm body under his. She clung to him.

'I love you,' he said.

When the fire had passed out of their bodies and their loving was over she lay in the hollow of his shoulder, caressing the muscles of his arm. He held her lightly and tenderly to him, as one holds a flower.

'Why did you stay away?' she asked.

'You did not want me.'

'That's not true. I hurt you that first time.'

'It was nothing.'

'I did. And when I came back you did not understand how I wanted you to take me.'

'You did. . . . Why?'

She laughed softly.

'Leah is right. You are a fool with people.'

'Why did you come for me to take you?'

'O you foolish one! I just wanted you.'

'I love you.'

'I know.'

'I did from the start.'

She traced a circle on his chest.

'Did you know that?'

'I am no good for you, Xuma.'

'Nonsense!'

'It is true. There is a devil in me that wants things I cannot get.'

'You are beautiful.'

'It is good when you say it so.'

'But it is true.'

'I love you, Xuma.'

She snuggled closer and went to sleep.

EIGHT

Xuma woke slowly, reluctantly, from his deep and peaceful sleep. He stretched out his hand, feeling for Eliza. All through the night he had been conscious of her there beside him. A movement. A sigh. Childlike mutterings in her sleep. Nestling closer to him. All these little things had forced her presence on him while he slept. And it had made his sleep deep and blissful.

He had woken once in the night and had listened to the evenness of her breathing. And a great tenderness and protectiveness had stolen over his heart. He had covered her, then, with the sure, gentle touch of a mother covering an unprotected child.

He felt only the pillow. He sat up, suddenly wide awake. She was not there. Not in the bed and not in the room. Perhaps she had gone to make tea, he thought. But he knew it was not that. Where she had slept was cold. She must have gone a long time ago. He knew, without knowing how or why, that she had gone and would not come back to the room.

He got up and dressed.

Outside the sun was shining, but it was a cold, ineffectual sun that could not dispel the sharp coldness of the air.

'Morning, Xuma,' Ma Plank called. 'Did you sleep well?'

'Very well,' Xuma said. 'And you?'

'I was just bringing you some coffee,' Maisy called from the kitchen window.

'Thank you, I will come and get it,' Xuma said.

He washed himself under the tap in the yard. The cold water bit him.

'There is some hot water here,' Maisy called.

'I have washed,' he replied.

Maisy laughed and there was the joy of a summer's morning in her voice. Xuma smiled and went into the kitchen.

'You look good,' Maisy said laughing at him with her eyes.

'I feel good,' he said.

'What's come over you?' Ma Plank asked. 'Last night you were sour and now you are like one who could jump over the sun, heh?'

'Maybe I could!'

With a long, lingering look Maisy gave him the mug of coffee.

'Yes, maybe he could,' she said.

'Where are the others?'

'Eliza's in her room,' Maisy said.

'Leah has gone to try and find out who is betraying us,' Ma Plank said.

Xuma emptied the mug and put it down.

'More?' Maisy asked.

'No.'

'Is she asleep?'

'No.'

Xuma crossed the room.

'Don't go,' Maisy said.

Xuma cocked his head and smiled. Maisy turned her back on him and looked out of the window. Xuma went through. He knocked on Eliza's door. There was no reply. He knocked again then went in.

Eliza turned her head from the wall and looked at him.

'Hello!' he said and tried to take her in his arms.

She pushed him away and shrank from him.

'No, Xuma!'

Xuma stopped and looked at her.

'What is it? Are you unwell my darling?'

'No! I don't want you to touch me.'

'But Eliza, only last night. . . .'

'I was a fool last night. Please leave me.'

'But . . .'

'Please go!'

'If you want the things of the white people, it is all right. We will save money and get them, heh?'

'Please go, Xuma!'

Xuma tried to speak again, but she pointed to the door.

'Go, please!'

Xuma clenched his fists and went out. Eliza buried her face in the pillow and sobs shook her body from head to feet.

Xuma went into the yard. Maisy followed him.

'I am sorry,' she said.

'It is nothing.'

He looked up at the sky. A cloud had covered the sun.

'I tried to warn you.'

She slipped her hand into his and squeezed it. He felt the hardness of her little hand. Not soft like the white woman's and the doctor's wife's and Eliza's. But it comforted him. He returned the pressure of her hand.

'You are kind,' he said.

'Not kind,' she said.

'Food is ready,' Ma Plank called.

They went in. Leah had returned. Her face looked pinched with cold. She looked stronger than ever, though.

'Did you find out anything?' Ma Plank asked.

'No. There is someone who betrays me. That is certain. I saw the one who gives me warning. They have questioned him closely and he is even afraid to talk to me. Yes, there is someone who betrays me but no one can tell me who he is. I met the inspector when I was returning and he told me he was going to get me.'

'Then don't sell for a little time,' Ma Plank said.

Leah snorted. 'And the sky will give us money, I suppose. I must start soon but before that I must catch the swine who is betraying me. And if I catch him . . .' She opened her hands then clenched them viciously.

'But how will you find out?'

'It is the same one who betrayed my man and who betrayed Joseph. That I know now. . . .'

The front door banged.

'Eliza,' said Ma Plank.

Xuma jumped up and hurried to the front door. Eliza was hurrying down the street. He called her but she went on, unheeding. He went back to the kitchen. He caught Maisy's eye.

'She's gone,' he said.

The joy of the night turned bitter in him. His longing for her was greater than it had ever been, for he had known her and found her very warm and very desirable. Now it was all black and painful.

'Eat!' Ma Plank rapped at him, but there was kindness in her eyes.

Maisy moved closer to him.

'I am going to some friends,' she said. 'I am not working today. Come with me. It will help you to forget. They are good people. It will be good for you.'

Her voice was soft and coaxing.

'Eat your food, Leah,' Ma Plank said.

'Where is Daddy?' Leah asked. 'Did you get a drink for him?'

'Yes. He's all right. He cannot move now, but the drink will warm him up soon and he will come and eat.'

'I will set a trap,' Leah said thoughtfully.

'Maybe it's that yellow one, Drunk Liz,' Ma Plank said.

'No.'

'I am sure it's not Johannes or Lena.'

'Of course not!'

'It will be good for you to come with me,' Maisy coaxed Xuma.

'You are a fool to bother with me,' he said. 'I am a fool to want Eliza – such a woman; and now you are a fool for bothering with me.'

'I know I am not a fool. Will you come with me?' Her voice and eyes were pleading with him.

It made him feel better that someone wanted him after the way Eliza had treated him. It was good to know that someone cared for him.

'I know she was with you all last night,' Maisy said.

He looked at her. She knew and yet she wanted him to go with her.

'You are a strange one,' he said.

She smiled and there was something dark behind the laughter in her eyes. She wanted to tell him that Eliza was no good for him but she knew it would be fatal. She knew the one thing she had to avoid was to talk about Eliza.

'Will you come? It is a long way off and we must catch the bus soon. You will like it. It is like being in the country there. There is grass on the ground and trees and there is a river and there are cows and farms. Will you come?'

He laughed. The way she described the place told him it was foreign to her to be away from the city.

'Why do you laugh?'

'Have you ever been on the farms?'

'No.'

'That is why I laugh. When you talk about it one can see it is strange to you.'

'Yes,' Leah told Ma Plank. 'I will set a trap for this dog.'

Maisy got up and went into another room. When she returned she had her hat and coat on. Her eyes asked him to come.

'Yes, I will come,' he said suddenly.

Maisy went out and fetched his hat and coat and helped him put them on.

'I am going to Hoopvlei and Xuma's coming too,' Maisy told Leah.

'All right,' Leah said absently.

Ma Plank followed them to the door.

Daddy came out of the room buttoning up the fly of his trousers. He was in the first stages of drunkenness.

'Leah is worried,' Ma Plank said. Then she smiled at them, 'Don't be too naughty.' She patted Maisy's bottom.

'Stop it, old woman!' Xuma said and laughed.

'Listen to him,' Ma Plank said and swung round neatly, at the same time smacking her bottom resoundingly. 'And he calls me old. I can do better than many a young filly. . . . And if ever you doubt it Xuma, come and find out!'

She pushed them off and stood laughing on the verandah.

Xuma looked at Maisy and smiled.

'She is funny.'

'She makes fun but she is good and very wise. She says nothing but she sees many things.'

At the corner they stopped and waved. Ma Plank waved back. Daddy stood beside her.

They hurried to the bus stop. The Hoopvlei bus was just moving away. Maisy sprinted after it and Xuma followed her. They jumped on.

The bus was crowded but they found room at the back. They sat pressed against each other. Xuma's arm dug into Maisy's side so he slipped it round her shoulders. She looked up at him and the laughter in her eyes flowed up to him, and for no reason they laughed.

Maisy said something but the din was so great that Xuma could not hear. He bent his head. She tried again. But still he could not hear. She opened her bag and took out a packet of cigarettes, took one and put it between his lips and lit it. Then she closed her eyes and went to sleep against his shoulder.

Xuma felt light-hearted suddenly. As he had felt that night when she had taken him to join the dancing ring. This one knew how to be happy. She knew how to laugh. And it was so good that she made other people laugh and be happy as well.

After two hours Maisy, who had slept fitfully, woke. She looked around to find their bearings.

'We are nearly there,' she said. 'We will get out a little way along and we will walk down. It is nice. You will like it.'

They got out two miles further. Maisy took his hand and led him along a footpath. They were in open country. It reminded him of the open of his home. The stillness and peace of it. And the good soft earth. Not hard, macadamized roads, but soft clinging earth.

'Now look,' Maisy said.

They had come round a bend. And below them was the valley and in the hollow of it nestled Hoopvlei – Valley of Hope – a cluster of houses and a few streets. And behind it ran the river.

'It is beautiful,' Xuma said and took a deep breath.

'I was sure you would like it,' Maisy said.

'It is the land, the earth, it is good,' Xuma said.

'Come,' Maisy said and ran down the footpath.

She ran nimbly and easily, jumping over stones and dodging jutting rock points. Xuma followed more slowly, sucking in the fresh air and looking around with hunger in his eyes. He had longed for the land more than he had known. And there it was now, stretches of it. And again the sky was close to the earth.

'Come on!' Maisy shouted.

'All right!' he yelled with joy.

Her clear, carefree laughter drifted to him. Yes, it was like home. He ran down the sloping footpath. When he was within a few yards of her Maisy dashed off.

'Catch me!' she called.

Xuma dashed after her, made a grab, but she evaded him and skipped away laughing.

'Catch me!'

'I will!'

He was feeling as he had felt that night when they had gone dancing, completely free and happy.

They chased down the sloping footpath, Maisy in front and Xuma close on her heels. Maisy ran easily and fast. Whenever he was close to her Xuma would put out his hand to grab her but she would be gone, and he would hear the peals of her merry laughter.

Xuma slackened his pace. Maisy did so too. Then suddenly Xuma shot forward. He grabbed her waist and they fell and tumbled in the grass.

They lay there panting and laughing, too hot to feel the cold air.

'You cheated,' Maisy said.

'My! but you can run.'

Maisy jumped up.

'We must go now, my friends will see the bus and think I'm not coming. Come.'

They walked down by the river. Xuma pitched pebbles into the river. Maisy danced to and away from him as she had done that evening they had gone dancing. Xuma was happy. She knew it. She had made him happy. He may run after Eliza, but twice he had been with her and twice he had been happy. He will remember that. Men are thus.

'It is like at home,' Xuma said. 'It is so because I am with you and you know the things that make a person happy.'

Maisy shot a quick glance at him. His eyes were on the ground and there was an empty, peaceful stare in them. She looked down river and quickened her pace.

Xuma walked more slowly, listening to the rushing of soft water over pebbles, watching the eddying pools where the flow of the water was interrupted by a jutting stone or by a willow branch that trailed in the water.

The sky was clear and distant, and yet a part of the earth and of the green grass on which he walked. If only Eliza were with him. If she were there to walk beside him. Perhaps to touch his hand. If that had been then all would have been perfect. But she had refused to speak to him that morning and had gone away. Maisy was the one who was good. She understood. He looked at her, way there ahead of him. She had taken off her coat and was carrying it on her arm. A cool breeze blew her dress and the outlines of her body were clear.

A good one, that. One who understands. And one who wanted him. Why not her? Why Eliza? She would not hurt him as Eliza had. And she knew the things that were good for him and she did those things.

'Maisy!'

She waited, looking very young and very desirable, and that light of laughter in her eyes.

He looked into her eyes. They laughed up at him and he smiled.

'You are good,' he said and slipped his arm round her waist.

He bent towards her. She leaned back and looked at his face. The laughter left her eyes and slowly she shook her head.

'No, Xuma. You are thinking of her, not of me.'

She freed herself and walked away, eyes studying the grass.

Xuma wanted to tell her that it was not so. But he knew she would know he was lying. He followed her.

They were near the little township now. They could see the houses clearly. And the people moving about in the yards and by the sides of the houses. This side of the township had mostly coloured people. The other side was where the native people were.

Hoopvlei was another of the white man's ventures to get the natives and coloureds out of the towns. The natives did not like the locations, and besides, they were all full, so the white man had started townships in the outlying district of Johannesburg in the hope of killing Vrededorp and Malay Camp. Many other places had been killed thus.

Perhaps in five or ten years Malay Camp would only be a name. And perhaps even Vrededorp, the heart-throb of the dark people of the city, would be like a dream told to a child who was sleepy, and who, on waking, would remember only vague snatches of it. Perhaps it would be so in five years' time.

They walked past the houses, past the working men and women

and past the playing children. A silence had grown between them. There had been silence before, but it had been the silence of understanding. This was the silence of strangers. Xuma felt he had done her wrong and did not know how to undo it. This he resented.

'Look!' Maisy exclaimed.

She ran to his side and took his arm and pointed. On the other side of the river a boy without a shirt was driving a herd of cows. Xuma laughed.

'You should belong to the farms,' he said.

'Don't you like it?'

'It is very good,' he said with laughter in his voice.

She looked up at him. The laughter of his voice was showing in his eyes too. Her eyes laughed back.

It was nearly midnight and the last taxi was crowded. Maisy had to sit on Xuma's knee. There were eight of them in the back seat of the taxi and it was hard to move.

The day had gone so quickly that before they knew it, it was time for the last bus. And then they missed it. Maisy's friends had been good. They were as full of laughter as Maisy and soon Xuma had felt that he had known them all his life.

They had behaved as though he were Maisy's man and Maisy had looked at him waiting for him to deny it but he had said nothing. They had given them beer, not as it was made in the city, but as it was made on the farm. And they had talked, and all the time Maisy had been close to him.

He had forgotten Eliza and Leah and Daddy and Ma Plank and the mines and everything connected with the city. And it seemed that Maisy was not connected with the city. And there had been laughter, free and happy as in the old days on the farms.

They had talked much of the farms for the man of Maisy's friend came from the farms and loved the farms much. He talked of going back to the farms when he had money to buy a piece of land. But when he did so his woman looked at him as one would look at a child playing with water.

And under the warmth of their friendliness and the freedom to talk that the beer had given him, and with his hand on Maisy's shoulder he talked about his home and his people. About the beauty of morning on the highveld when the sun came up and the

96

birds sang and the cattle called to be led out to pasture, and about the sweetness of his mother and the great strength of his father when he and his brother were young. And how they used to chase rabbits. He had told them all things he had done as a child and as a young man.

Then other people had come and more beer had flowed and there had been singing and much laughter and dancing. He had danced with people he had not known. He had spoken to them and they had spoken to him. And Maisy's friend had thrown her arm round his neck and made him carry her. And Maisy had laughed and thrown her arms round the neck of her friend's man. And all the people had clapped and laughed.

And men carried women in their arms and they made a ring and marched round the room till the room was too small and then they had gone into the yard.

And there they had made a ring and a woman had sung a song and the people in the ring had clapped and stamped their feet. And a man and a woman had gone into the centre of the ring. And they had danced.

And when they were tired more beer flowed and again they had danced. A man had brought a guitar and another a concertina. And from all round people had come. Women had brought food and beer and there had been much to eat and drink. And through it all had shone Maisy's laughing face and shining eyes. And Maisy was beside him, full of laughter and happiness and giving him laughter and happiness.

And in the middle of it all he had taken Maisy by the hand and they had walked down to the river in the moonlight. And for no reason they had laughed. And their laughter would not stop and rang out all along the river.

Then the others had come to find them so they hid themselves and it was a long time before the others found them. And when they did find them they carried them shoulder high and marched back to the house, singing.

And again there had been the flow of beer. And life was good for the beer was the beer of the farms and not the poison of the city that was only to make you drunk and not to make you happy.

And then Maisy had pulled him and shaken him and told him it was time for the bus. They had put on their overcoats and all the other people had gone with them to the bus stand. But the bus had gone and there was no other till morning.

Maisy's friend had said they should sleep at her place. But Maisy had said no and explained that he had to be at the mines very early. He had said it was nothing. He would stay. But Maisy had been firm and told him he was drunk. So they had more beer.

Then they had found the last taxi.

And now Maisy was sitting on his lap in a crowded taxi. He was sorry it was over. It had been good. He had wanted it to go on. Maisy slipped her arm round his neck. It made him feel better.

The taxi shot away and raced through the night, towards Johannesburg. This time the journey took only an hour.

When they got out Xuma did not know where he was and did not care.

'I am drunk,' he told Maisy.

'I will look after you,' she said and took his arm.

He smiled. With Maisy to look after him he could come to no harm. He was sure of that.

After a little while she led the way down a passage and made him wait while she opened a door. Then she pulled him into a little room. She shut the door and switched on the light. He looked at the electric bulb. The white man's light.

'Where is this?'

'My room. This is the place where I work. It is better for you to sleep here, I can wake you in time in the morning.'

He went over to the bed and sat down. He looked round the room. It looked like the white man's room. But he was not sure. He could not see straight. Everything moved. It was as though his head moved. He clutched it with both hands and tried to steady it. Still it would not stop.

'Lie down,' Maisy said.

He obeyed her. It was better, things did not move so much. But now it was hard to keep his eyes open.

'Maisy.'

'Heh?'

'Come here.'

She went to him. He held out his hand. She took it and patted it.

'You will not leave me.'

98

'No.'

'You will look after me.'

'Yes, I will look after you.'

'That is good,' Xuma said and went to sleep.

Maisy undressed him, then made a bed for herself on the floor. For a minute she stood looking at him, then she turned out the light.

NINE

'Wake up! Xuma! Wake up!'

He rolled over and opened his eyes.

'But it is dark still,' he complained.

'You must go to work,' Maisy said.

Xuma sat up and rubbed his eyes. He remembered last night. He was in Maisy's room. He had been out with Maisy all yesterday. There was a slight throb in his head, but the beer had been good and it was not bad.

'Get dressed. I will bring you food,' Maisy said and went out.

Xuma dressed and studied the room. It was a nice room, a woman's room. He saw the bed on the floor.

Maisy came in with a mug of steaming coffee and bread and meat on a plate.

'Did you sleep there?' he asked pointing to the bed on the floor.

She nodded.

'You must hurry,' she said.

'What is the time?'

'It is five. . . . You must go to your room to get your working clothes.' He nodded. He had not thought of it.

'Why did you sleep on the floor?'

'Don't sit there talking, hurry.'

She had brought in a bowl of water. He washed, then ate. When he had finished he got up and stood looking at her. It was hard to understand her. She had wanted him and when she had got him she slept on the floor.

'You have been good to me,' he said.

'Come,' she said.

He followed her out through the little passage. The morning was cold. The coffee was comfortably warm in his belly.

'You go down this road till where it turns to the left. Follow the turning and it will bring you to Malay Camp.'

He did not want to go. He looked at Maisy's face. She had not looked at him all this time. Now she raised her eyes and looked at him and the laughter was there with the sleepiness.

'Yesterday was good,' he said and took her hand.

'I am glad.'

'You are a good one. Maybe we will go there again, heh?'

'If you want it.'

'I do want it.'

'Now go or you will be late.'

Her hand was cold. Through her hand he could feel her body shivering. She had had no coffee.

'Good-bye,' he said.

'Good-bye.'

But it was hard to leave her just like that. Something else had to be done, but he did not know what it was. She freed her hand.

'Go.'

He walked a few yards then stopped and looked back. She had gone in. He hurried down the wide, tree-lined road. The coldness in the air was sharp. He pushed his hands deep into his pockets and turned up the collar of his overcoat. It would be good underground on a day like this. But it would be even better to be sitting round a blazing fire such as there would be at Leah's today.

At his room he changed then set out for the mines.

At the mine gates he met Johannes.

'Hi there! Sonofabitch Xuma!'

Xuma smiled. Johannes was still drunk. Not very drunk but not sober.

'How is it, Johannes?'

'I'm J. P. Williamson, me! Strong as an ox and I'm going to break their jail. You will see!'

Xuma took his arm and they passed through the gate.

'What is wrong.'

'It is a shame, brother Xuma.'

'Tell me, what is it?'

'They've taken my woman.'

'Taken your woman – Lena?'

'Yes! Sonofabitch police. I will kill one!'

'Why?'

'Seven days or a pound.'

'Why did they take her?'

'Drunk and noisy.'

'Don't worry, we will try to get the money and get her out. Maybe Leah will lend it to you. I will ask her and you can pay it back later, heh?'

'No!' Johannes roared.

'Don't shout,' Xuma said.

'It will be good for the sonofabitch. Let her work for the seven days!'

'Then why do you want to break the jail?'

Johannes flung his arm round Xuma's shoulder and smiled.

'I don't know, brother,' he whispered.

Xuma led Johannes to the tap and made him wash his face. Johannes protested that the water was too cold but Xuma forced him and amid much swearing Johannes washed.

The long column of marching mine boys from the compound came round the bend, led and flanked by indunas. Their feet made a dull noise on the ground and they left a trail of fine dust in their wake.

Paddy and another white man came out of the shack where the white men rested and had their tea. He saw Xuma and called him. Xuma left Johannes at the tap and went to the shack.

'Ho Zuma!'

'Ho Red One.'

'How is it?'

'It is good.'

'I see you are helping Johannes to sober up. Is he very drunk?'

Xuma remained silent. Paddy smiled and offered him a cigarette.

'Listen Zuma, we will work till it is food time then we will come up and there will be no more work for us till it is midnight. And after that we will work at night only. This will be for a month. Is it clear?'

'It is clear.'

'Good. You will tell your boys.'

102

Xuma turned and walked away.

'I say, Xuma!'

Xuma turned back. It was Chris. He had just come out of the shack.

'Yes?'

'Tell Johannes we will not go down till it is time for you to come up and explain the new shifts to him, will you?'

A column of men marched from the right. They marched out of the gate and round the bend in the road on their way to the compound. Johannes was still standing with his head under the cold water. Engines hummed. Indunas shouted orders. A gang of men stood at the entrance of the cages that would shoot them downward into the bowels of the earth in search of gold.

Xuma went over to Johannes.

'Your white man says you will not work till it is time to eat.'

Johannes was sobering. He looked less like J. P. Williamson. Xuma took his arm.

'New shifts?'

'Yes.'

'How do they work?'

Xuma explained.

'Then I will go and sleep a little,' Johannes said.

'Is it true about your woman?' Xuma asked.

'Yes.'

'Then we will try and get the money from Leah.'

'No. I owe too many people. I still owe Leah some money too.'

Johannes seemed ashamed of himself, ashamed of having been drunk, of his great size, of the fact that he owed people money.

'Go to my room,' Xuma said. 'Here is the key. Sleep there till it is time to come. You will find bread, and there is also a tin of sardines. Eat them. It will be good for you.'

Johannes bit his lower lip and looked away. Xuma had been at the mines for only a short time but Xuma had a room of his own and food and clothes and he owed nobody any money.

Xuma looked at Johannes and understood what was going on in his mind. He punched Johannes on the chest.

'Are we not friends, heh?'

'Thank you,' Johannes said and turned away.

His men were waiting for Xuma. The cage had come up. It was time to go down. Johannes walked a little way then stopped and came back.

'I saw Dladla,' Johannes said. 'He had much money and was drunk and boastful. He said Leah would be sorry for what she did to him. He said her man and Joseph were sorry and she would be too. Maybe he is betraying her to the police. When you see her warn her.'

'I will,' Xuma said.

So it was Dladla. Why had they not thought of that?

'I knocked him down and he went to sleep,' Johannes said as if apologizing.

'That was good.'

An induna called him so Xuma hurried off to the waiting cage. The men waited. As he came up they greeted him.

'All right!' Xuma said.

The men filed into the cage.

'That's enough,' Xuma called. 'Move!'

The cage moved slowly downward. Another empty cage took its place.

'All right!'

More men filed in.

'Enough! Move!'

He was master here, the one who gave the orders, the one who looked after the men. He was sure of himself. Sure of his strength. Sure of his control over the men. Sure of their respect for him.

A group of white men stood nearby, watching. Xuma was the best mine boy in that mine. And his team had become the best under him. And that meant that Paddy's money had gone up. So the white men watched with respect.

'Lucky blighter,' one said to Paddy.

Paddy nodded.

'You should give him a weekly tip of a quid,' another said.

The third cage filled up. Xuma waited for Paddy. Paddy hurried forward. Xuma was the last to get in. That was as it should be. The boss boy looked after everyone, saw that everyone was safely in, then gave the signal then jumped as the cage began to move. That was the duty of the head mine boy.

The cages shot down. Down. Down. Down.

The men were silent. It was always so. Going into the bowels of the earth forced silence on them. And their hearts pounded. Many had gone in day after day for months. But they did not get used to it. Always there was the furious pounding of the hearts. The tightness in the throat. And the warm feeling in the belly. It was so for the mine boy. They knew it.

Only of the white man were they not sure. For the white man never showed anything. He never showed fear. He was never upset. He gave the orders and he was in front with the boss boy. And if it was a good boss boy, like Xuma or Johannes, then the boss boy too showed no fear and was never upset and gave the orders. That too was so. That too they knew.

Down shot the cages. Down. Down. Down.

And their lamps flickered and there was a thin, sharp whistle through the air as the cages shot down. Deep down into the body of the earth. And the only light was the light of their lamps. And the air became warmer and breathing seemed heavy. That too was always so.

The cages slowed down and the men jumped out. They stood around in groups, waiting.

Xuma walked beside Paddy. Paddy looked at his little book. Together they went to look over the place where they were going to work. The others waited near the cages. It was the duty of the white man and the boss boy to find out whether it was safe to work. It was their duty to see if everything was in order.

Another cage came down. There were four white men in it. They stood a little away from the others and waited for Paddy and Xuma.

Xuma studied the sides and roof of the tunnel as they went along. Where the tunnel led to the wall where the working had to be, props had been built to look like the frame-work of a doorway. The roof of this sagged. Xuma studied it for a long time. Paddy who had gone ahead came back and stood beside him.

'What do you think?' Paddy asked.

'Maybe it is nothing,' Xuma said, 'but I think we should put two more stout poles on each side.'

Paddy nodded. 'Yes, and perhaps one cross-wise against the roof, heh?'

'Good.'

'Otherwise?'

'It is all right.'

Paddy went to a phone that had been strung along to keep touch with the surface.

'All right for power,' he called into the mouthpiece.

Xuma walked down the tunnel and called the others. The four white men walked ahead. They passed Xuma. The native boys stopped in front of him. He looked them over and selected the four strongest.

'You will get poles and build up this place,' he told them.

They went off to get the poles.

'Come,' Xuma told the others and led them down to where Paddy was.

Paddy gave the four white men their places to work. Xuma sorted out the boys and gave each white man ten.

The four boys brought the poles and began to build up the weak side of the tunnel.

'Right,' Paddy said and smiled at Xuma.

'To work!' Xuma called and moved among the men.

Here he helped one. There he showed one the best way of digging. At another place he showed how best to put a boulder on the conveyor belt.

Paddy walked from one white man to the other, watching them drill and marking places that look like possible gold seams.

The drill hummed. The hammer rang. There was a swish and a buzz and a hum, and there was the clang of the pick and grating of the shovel. And slowly the rhythm of the work gathered pace.

Xuma smiled. He knew the rhythm. He controlled it. He kept up its steady pace. He was master, with the Red One, of this spot. He gave the orders and he knew the Red One would not contradict him for the Red One knew the wisdom of his orders.

Paddy took a drill, switched it on and held it to the side of the wall of rock. The muscles of his arms and chest rippled under the hum of the drill. Xuma turned from a group of boys and took another drill. He stepped beside Paddy and put the drill to the rock wall. The muscles of his arms and chest also rippled under the hum of the drill. They worked shoulder to shoulder. Two strong men. A white man and a black.

And the conveyor belt sang and the picks fell and the spades grated and the drills hummed. And everywhere men worked. Their bodies streaming with sweat. . . .

And in Xuma's mind there was room for nothing but his work. Without stopping he would turn his head and call to a man to do this or that or he would warn one who was lingering or he would tell one to leave what he was doing and do something else. And, perhaps, he would look up and catch Paddy's eye, and the Red One would be smiling through his teeth while between them they broke the wall of rock.

And an ever-rising stream of shining rocks and pebbles and fine dust would travel upwards to be sifted, crushed and sorted for the fine yellow metal men love and call gold. . . .

One of the men who had been putting up the poles at the weak spot in the tunnel tapped Xuma's shoulder. Xuma stopped his drilling and turned.

'There is water coming through,' the man shouted.

Xuma followed him to the place. He looked up. It was damp and a thin trickle of water seeped through. Xuma called Paddy and showed him the place. Paddy studied it for a little while then went to the phone and shouted for an engineer to come and look at it.

The engineer came down, looked at it, examined it, and said it was safe. Paddy looked at Xuma's face and saw the doubt there. He asked the engineer whether he was certain. The engineer was very firm in his certainty. They went back to their work.

And gold dust streamed upwards to make men wealthy and powerful.

When the hour to eat came the men flung their tools from them and stood around with weariness on their faces and sweat dripping from their bodies. Xuma called them together and told them about the new shifts. Without seeming to care they hurried towards the cages.

A man near Xuma coughed. A trickle of red spittle flew out of his mouth and fell at Xuma's feet. Xuma stared at it. He had heard about the sickness of the lungs and how it ate a man's body away, but he had never seen a man who had it. He looked at the man. The man's eyes shone brightly and his nostrils quivered. He was an old man.

'Come here,' Xuma said.

The man stepped forward. All the others waited and there was fear in their eyes. Xuma felt fear shooting through his body. The man in front of him was still a man. But the signs were there already. He was bony. He was a man who had been big and muscular once and this showed in his boniness.

'You can go,' Xuma said to the others.

They went slowly, reluctantly. When they had gone Xuma spoke to the man:

'How long have you had this?'

'Two months now,' the man said.

'Did you see the doctor?'

'No,' the man said and hung his head.

'Why not?'

The man looked at the ground and fidgeted with his hands.

'Listen, Xuma, I have a wife and two children and I have worked it all out. We have a small farm and I owe a white man eight pounds. If I do not give it back to him he will take the farm. And if he takes it, where will my wife and children go? I have worked it all out, Xuma, really I have. For four months I have been saving and if I save for another three months I will have the eight pounds and there will be a home for my wife and children. Please let me stay. Don't tell the white people. The others will not. They know. I know I am going to die, but if there is a home for my wife and children I will be happy.'

'And that is why you did not tell of your sickness?'

'That is why.' Xuma felt the fear hammering at his heart.

'What is it, Zuma?'

It was Paddy. He stood a few yards away. Xuma remained silent so Paddy came closer. Paddy looked at the man closely. There was blood at the side of the man's mouth. The man began to cough painfully. Paddy nodded.

'You must see the doctor.'

'No!' the man said.

'Tell him,' Xuma said to the man.

The man told Paddy about his wife and two children and about the eight pounds. When he had finished Paddy turned away and walked to where they had been working. After a little while he came back.

'Did not the man who hired you tell you that if you got the sickness of the chest money would be paid to you?'

'No.'

'Well, it is so,' Paddy said.

The man looked at Xuma. His eagerness was painful.

'Is that so, Xuma?'

Xuma did not know. He looked at Paddy. He hesitated, then nodded.

'Yes, it is so.'

'That is good,' the man said, 'now they will have a home. That is good.'

'Go to the doctor,' Paddy said. 'We will come and everything will be all right.'

The man went. Xuma looked at Paddy.

'Is it true that he will get money?' There was doubt in Xuma's voice.

'Yes, it is true. Come, you will see.' They followed the man into the last cage. The cage shot up. Up. Up. Up.

The other shift was ready and waiting for them. Johannes returned Xuma's keys to him. He was quite sober. There were dark rings under his eyes and his hands trembled.

Paddy stood talking to Chris for a minute, then he called Xuma and they went to the hospital. Xuma waited outside with the man while Paddy went in and spoke to the doctor.

Then the doctor called them in and examined the man. The examination was short. There was no doubt about it. The doctor wrote out a slip and gave it to Paddy.

And again Xuma and the man followed Paddy as he went to the mine manager's office. They waited outside. It seemed a long time. Then the manager came out with Paddy. He grumbled about it being irregular but signed a piece of paper and gave it to Paddy.

'There you are!' Paddy exclaimed. 'Now we will go and get the money and then you can go home.'

The man's lips trembled when he smiled.

They got the money from the cashier. Ten pounds and a full month's wages, three pounds five. That made it thirteen pounds and five shillings. They also got a free railway warrant to the man's home and a pass to show that he was not escaping from the mines. Paddy gave him all this.

'The doctor wants you to go to the hospital but you are also free to go home,' Paddy said.

'Any time?'

'Yes, any time.'

'Even today?'

'Yes, even today.'

The man clenched his fists to steady himself. He looked at Paddy, then at Xuma and smiled. His eyes shone.

'You are a good man, Red One. And you too, Xuma, you are a real brother. The Great One will look after you. ... Now there will be a home for my wife and children and I will be with them for a short space. That is good.'

The man saluted them and walked away. The other boys were waiting for him. He told them the good news. And in his joy he pushed out his chest and called out a battle-cry that ended on a painful, lung-tearing cough. The man and his friends joined the column that was going to the compound. It was his last march. Soon he would be with his wife and children. Soon the debt would be paid. . . .

'That was a good thing you did,' Xuma said to Paddy.

'A good thing,' Paddy said bitterly.

Abruptly he walked away and left Xuma standing alone. Xuma stood there for a little while then he went to the wash place. Down the road the tail of the column of marching men disappeared round the bend.

Xuma changed his clothes and looked round the room. He smiled. A strange one, that Johannes. Who would have thought that he would have made the bed and swept the floor and left everything clean and tidy. A strange one, yes.

And the Red One had done a very good thing for the sick man. He went out and locked the door behind him. There was the whole day, the whole afternoon in front of him. He did not feel tired or sleepy at all. Perhaps later on he would sleep a little, but now he wanted to go out.

He wondered whether he should go to Leah's place. But if he went there he would have to tell her about Dladla. And he had seen Leah's hands open and close and the look on her face when she had spoken about the one who was betraying her. He did not want to tell her about Dladla.

'I will go to Maisy,' he told himself.

110

He wondered whether she would be busy or whether she would be afraid in case her white people saw him. But he felt sad and he knew that Maisy was the only one who could cheer him up. Leah would understand but Leah could not cheer him up. Only Maisy could for Maisy knew how.

When he got to the broad tree-lined street he was not sure of the house. He had not looked closely that morning. It was somewhere here, he decided. And there was a passage. But all the other houses had passages and they all looked the same.

He slackened his pace outside the house that seemed to be the one. How could he find out? One did not go to white people's places and ask if Maisy worked there.

A little boy ran out of the passage. Could he ask the little boy? Maybe he'd better not. Some of these boys were naughty and if the boy cried there would be trouble for him.

'Hello,' the boy said.

Xuma smiled. This was a good little one. He could ask him.

'Hello,' Xuma said.

'What's your name?' the boy asked.

'Xuma.'

'What?'

'Xuma.'

'That's a funny name.'

'Johnny!' a voice called from the yard.

'That is Maisy,' Johnny said. 'She wants me to have tea but I don't want to have tea. Do you want to have tea?'

Xuma did not know what to say so he smiled. So it was Maisy's place.

'Come on, Johnny.'

It was another voice this time.

'That's my mother,' Johnny said. 'She wants me to have tea. Do you want to have tea?'

Again Xuma smiled. He wondered what Maisy's white woman was like. The gate opened and Maisy's white woman came out and behind her was Maisy.

'Xuma!' Maisy exclaimed when she saw him. 'Did you not go to the mines?'

She did not seem to mind her white woman.

'Yes. I have finished for the day. I start again at twelve tonight.'

'I see.'

'Come and have your tea, Johnny,' the white woman said to the child.

'I don't want tea,' the child said.

'Do you want to grow as big as Maisy's friend?' the woman asked.

'Oo yes!' the child said.

'Then you must have your tea.'

'Do you have tea?' the child asked Xuma.

'Yes,' Xuma said and nodded vigorously.

'There you are!' the woman said. 'Maisy's going to give her friend tea too.'

'Are you going to give him tea?' the child asked Maisy.

'Yes.'

'And some of mummy's cookies?'

'Of course,' his mother said.

'All right,' the child said and followed his mother.

'I was not sure this was your place,' Xuma said.

'I am glad you came,' Maisy said.

'And your white woman?'

'She is good. Come inside.'

Xuma followed her into the little room where he had spent the night before.

'Have you eaten?' Maisy asked.

'Yes.'

'You will have tea?'

'Yes.'

Maisy went for the tea. Xuma sat on the bed. Already he felt better. With Maisy it was so. She understood him and made him feel better. But he could not get the man who had spat blood out of his mind. He could still hear the cough and see the look in the man's eyes.

Maisy came back with the tea and with some of mummy's cookies.

'The white woman sends these,' Maisy said and smiled.

Xuma returned her smile. It was thus with Maisy. She laughed and one had to return her laugh. And when she smiled one had to do so too. There was a warmness in her that showed in the laughter of her eyes and it warmed a person.

112

Maisy gave him a cup of tea.

'What is it? You look sad.'

'I saw one who spat blood,' he said and told her about the man who had a wife and two children and owed eight pounds.

'And that makes you sad?'

'I don't know. The man was going to die and he was happy because he had money to pay for the home of his wife and children.'

'And it makes you sad?' she asked again.

Xuma looked at her without knowing what to say.

'You are very good, Xuma, and I like you very much,' she said softly looking steadily at him.

Xuma saw the tenderness in her eyes and looked away.

'I like you too, Maisy, very much, but . . .'

Maisy smiled. 'Yes, I know.'

'No you don't! You think I want to like her but it is not so. She is no good for me and I know. But I cannot help myself. She is like a devil in me. I stayed away because I know she is like a devil in me.'

'And the ways of white folks are like a devil in her.'

'Yes.'

'I am sorry, Xuma.'

'But I do like you, Maisy. You are the one who makes me laugh. When I feel heavy I come to you. You are the good one and I know it. But if that one smiled at me I would go sick with longing for her.'

Maisy looked out of the window.

'You are tired, Xuma, lie down.'

Xuma stretched himself on the bed and closed his eyes. He felt better for having spoken to Maisy. That feeling that he was cheating her was not so strong now.

For a long time there was silence between them. Maisy sat staring out of the window. Xuma lay with closed eyes, a great sense of peace over him. Then he remembered Dladla.

'Dladla is betraying Leah,' he said without opening his eyes.

'Dladla? How do you know?'

'Johannes told me. He was drunk last night and boasted to Johannes.'

'Leah knows?'

'No.'

There was another stretch of silence between them. Maisy got up from where she sat near the window and walked over to the bed. She stood there looking down at him. He opened his eyes and looked at her.

'I will hurry up and finish my work and then we will go and warn Leah.'

'You saw her when she swore to get the one who betrayed her?'

'We must tell her. Now close your eyes and go to sleep. You must rest or you will be tired tonight when you start work. Close them.'

Maisy touched his forehead with cool soothing fingers. They lingered there for a second or so then she pulled them away.

'Go to sleep,' she repeated and went out, shutting the door behind her.

TEN

It was dusk on a winter evening as they walked through the streets on their way to Malay Camp to warn Leah. They had spoken very little. Maisy was quiet and subdued in her manner. The joy and laughter that was usually with her was not there. Xuma walked beside her.

As they drew near the place Eliza was there in his mind again. She had been out of his mind since he and Maisy had gone to Hoopvlei on Sunday morning and he had felt peaceful and happy. But there had been something lacking in his happiness. And he knew now that at the back of his mind had been the knowledge that it was Maisy and not Eliza who was giving him this happiness.

He had wanted it to be Eliza. For it was Eliza he wanted. If only Eliza laughed as Maisy did, danced as Maisy did, went out with him as Maisy did, he would have been happy. He could work hard and get things that would make a place where they live look like the white man's. But she was not like Maisy. She did not laugh. She did not dance. And he wished he did not love her so. He looked at Maisy and wished he loved her. But it was Eliza he loved and longed for.

'Maisy.'

'Yes?'

'Why is that when you love a person it is so?'

'Maybe you love the wrong person,' Maisy said, looking away. 'But maybe you cannot help it.'

'I know. I cannot help it. . . . And she?'

'I don't know.'

'Why don't you talk to her?'

'It is hard. With you I can talk. With her it is not so.'

'She came to you that night ... I mean, did you ask her to come?'

'I did not ask her. She came.'

'She loves you, Xuma.'

'How can it be?' he asked looking sharply at her.

'People are so, Xuma.'

'You are not so.'

'I am not Eliza. And you do not love me.'

'And you?'

Maisy raised her eyes to his face. Her mouth twisted into a bitter smile but laughter shone from her eyes. She shook her head slowly.

'You do love me?' Xuma persisted.

'What is it to you?'

Xuma watched the neon lights with their multi-coloured advertisements flashing on and off in the distance.

'It is much to me,' he said. 'It is much to me that you love me for you are a good person and I can understand you and talk to you.'

'And what is it for me? Is it good for me to watch you while you run after her? Is it good to see you come to me only when she chases you from her? And you tell me it is good that I should love you. Walk on your own!'

Maisy crossed the road and hurried down a side street. Xuma tried to follow her but the traffic and the stream of people blocked his way. He stood on the kerbside for a little while. Eliza was always angry with him. And now Maisy was angry too.

He shrugged and slowly made his way to Leah's place.

Leah was alone and she was slightly drunk and her eyes sparkled happily. She wore a gay blue dress with red and white flowers and she wore a many-coloured kerchief round her head. Her face shone with the fat she had rubbed in after her wash. On each ear dangled a long glass ear-ring, and a string of small glass beads circled her strong, handsome neck. She was pretty as she stood on the verandah, prettier than Xuma had ever seen her. And she stood there for everyone to see her big strong beauty.

Xuma stopped and stared at her in admiration.

'My! But you are good to look at!'

Leah laughed. A deep, happy, strong laugh.

'Have you seen my shoes?' she asked boastfully.

'No. Let me see?'

She stepped on to the pavement and displayed them. They were black, shining, low-heeled shoes, and they were new.

'Good?'

'Yes!'

'Let me see, Leah,' the woman from across the street called.

Leah stepped into the street.

'Come and look at Leah's new clothes!' the woman called.

People came out and called others. The people who lived in all the houses around came out to look at Leah's new clothes. To let them see better Leah strolled up and down the street, imitating the fashionable white ladies of Johannesburg. She swayed her hips and tried to glide. The people roared with joy. Stylishly she put her left hand on her hip and held an imaginary cigarette-holder in her right, flicking off imaginary ash and smiling in a superior, white manner.

Drunk old Daddy came rolling down the street. He saw Leah. His eyes opened in astonishment, then suddenly lighted up. He pulled himself erect and looked very haughty. He straightened an imaginary tie, flicked himself with imaginary gloves, and twirled an imaginary cane. He looked from side to side, cleared his throat, and, walking in a more or less straight line, went up to Leah and bowed from the waist in comic-opera fashion. Still flicking her imaginary cigarette, Leah gave the barest nod and languidly offered him her hand. With many flourishes he went on his knees and kissed the outstretched hand. In getting up the beer got the better of his nobility and he sprawled face down in the street. People laughed and clapped. Xuma held his sides and tears streamed from his eyes. Further away, Maisy, who had just arrived, sat helplessly in the gutter.

Without moving a muscle of her face Leah stood over Daddy, her hand still outstretched. Every inch the haughty lady. Daddy got up, straightened the ghost tie, flicked himself with the unseen gloves, twirled the non-existent cane and again bowed from the waist.

Then, with the utmost dignity, Leah took his arm. He doffed a hat that was not there, and, arm in arm, the lady flicking her cigarette, the gentleman twirling his cane and somehow managing to be steady on his legs, they strolled up and down the street.

The people laughed and shouted and clapped. But the grand lady and gentleman did not notice them. Every now and then the lady or gentleman would nod. And they would smile stiff superior smiles and make their turn with little flourishes, the lady flicking her cigarette and the gentleman twirling his stick. And then, in a thunder of applause, they went into the house, still the lady and gentleman.

Leah came out a few minutes later and told the people the lady and gentleman had gone off and invited everybody to a party. The people applauded the invitation loudly and went into their homes to get out their best clothes.

Maisy got up and went to Xuma.

'Did you tell her about Dladla?' she asked.

'No.'

'I will tell her,' she said.

Xuma looked down the street. Eliza had just turned the corner. She was coming up slowly. Maisy followed his look and saw. She turned away abruptly and went into the house. Xuma stayed on the verandah, watching Eliza coming up the street.

He wanted to go and meet her but he dared not. She was beautiful, coming up the street like that, head held high, her body swaying slightly as she moved. She was everything he wanted his woman to be. He could stand there and watch her for ever if she would always move like that. He could watch her pushing breasts and sturdy legs all his life.

Eliza saw him and waved. Xuma could not believe his eyes. It could not be true. But she had waved. He jumped off the verandah, an eager smile on his lips. But he did not go to her. He waited. She waved again. Yes! It was for him. He hurried forward. She smiled up at him. He took her hand.

'Hello Xuma. It is good to see you. You are not angry with me any more, are you?' Her voice was soft and sweet.

It was good to look into her eyes and see the warmness in them for him.

'I was not angry,' he said.

'I made you unhappy,' she said.

'It was nothing,' he said. 'Let me carry your bag.'

118

He took the bag from her. She smiled and slipped her arm through his. She leaned towards him a little and looked at him. And there was warmth and love in her eyes and Xuma was happy. Everything else was forgotten. Eliza was close to him, leaning on his arm and he could feel the warmth of her body and there was softness in her voice. What did it matter if she had hurt him in the past. She was with him and was leaning against him now and there was a smile on her lips and a light in her eyes. Now was all that mattered. Not yesterday and the things of yesterday.

'It was nothing,' he repeated firmly.

Eliza patted his hand.

'It was a bad thing,' she said.

'No,' he said. 'If a man loves a woman he loves her. That is all. There is no bad and there is no good. There is only love. The only thing that is bad is if a man loves a woman and she loves him not. Then it is bad. But if the man loves the woman and the woman loves the man then there cannot be a bad thing. And I love you so it cannot be bad if you love me.'

He waited, looking at her anxiously. Her eyes softened when she saw the anxious look in his eyes. She held his arm tightly.

'If a man loves a woman and she loves him not, why is it bad?'

'Because a man is not happy then.'

'Perhaps the woman is no good for him.'

'Maybe. But when a man loves he loves.'

'And you will be happy if I love you?'

They stopped outside the house. Xuma looked at Eliza and in his eyes she saw the answer to her question. It was there and it was so powerful that she could not take her eyes from his. It carried her along as he had carried her along on Saturday night. And they seemed to be alone in the world. Just the two of them in the big world.

'You did not ask me and I came to you on Saturday. Why was it? And I fight with you always. Why is it? And when you are not there I want you. Why is that? It is ever so with a man and his woman. You are a man. You should know. Listen, Xuma, I am your woman. If I want it or not it is so. I cannot help it. I am just your woman. But you must be strong with me for I am bad.'

She clung to his arm. Her lips trembled into a smile and tears shone in her eyes.

'Those things you want, what of them? The things of the white man and a man who can read books and talk in the white man's language with you? The things I can give you if I work hard, maybe. But I cannot read books and speak the white man's language. Heh?'

'It is madness,' she said and lowered her head. 'It is my madness and when it comes do not let me hurt you, leave me alone and when it is gone I will be good again. When it comes just go away and when you return it will be gone. I do love you, Xuma. I am your woman. I want it.' There were tears in her voice.

But her eyes were clear when she looked up at him again. The tears were gone and the shadows were gone and they told him that she loved him. Xuma gathered her in his arms and held her tight.

'It is good,' he said with the strength of the victorious male. He smiled down into Eliza's face and she smiled up into his.

People passing in the street looked at them standing there leaning against each other, looking at each other and their eyes softened and they nodded knowingly and went on their way.

'Life is good!' Xuma said.

He wanted to shout it at the top of his voice. To tell everybody everywhere that life is good.

'Yes,' Eliza said.

'You are beautiful,' he said.

'No . . .' she said and lowered her eyes.

'But it is true,' he insisted. 'That first time when I saw you I looked at you and said in my heart, she is beautiful. She is the most beautiful one I have ever seen. It is true.'

'The eyes of a lover tell lies,' she said.

'That is a lying proverb,' he said.

They laughed and he realized that it was the first time he had heard Eliza laugh and that her laughter was good. Like the ringing of very many soft, melodious bells.

'We must go in,' she said and looked at the street.

Two little boys stood there watching them, scornful amusement on their faces.

Maisy came out. She took everything in with one sharp look.

'Food is ready,' she said.

Xuma and Eliza followed her into the house.

The others were at table. It was a hurried meal for people had already started coming for the party.

Leah looked at Xuma and Eliza and gave one snorting laugh, loud and raucous.

'So! They have come together at last – the dog and the bitch. That is good. It is finished now. I was getting tired of it. Well! What are you standing there for? Eat! Because you love is no reason why you should hold up my party.'

Eliza drew Xuma to a bench.

'She means good,' Eliza said. 'Do not worry about her tongue.'

'I know,' Xuma said.

Leah got up and looked at Maisy. For a second her eyes softened, then the softness was gone. She slipped her arm round Maisy's shoulders and held her affectionately.

'Come, Maisy,' Leah said softly, 'there is work for us and much fun. You will be the head of the party. You will lead the dances and you will start the party and all the orders will be yours, heh?'

'That will be very good,' Ma Plank said.

'But I want to start the party,' Eliza said.

'Look after your man, teacher!' Leah said harshly and led Maisy out into the yard where people stood laughing and talking and where the music was tuning up.

'You must be happy tonight,' Leah told Maisy.

'I am happy,' Maisy said and hugged her.

'Go then, start the dancing. And laugh, my child for your laughter is good. It will make the others laugh too. Go!'

Maisy went forward and held up her hands. The people stopped talking and the music was hushed. She stood under a lamp that had been strung up on the wash line and told them they had to forget their troubles and be happy for happiness was good. Then she sang a song of happiness. The guitar and the banjo and the concertina joined her. The people hummed. The music was warm and cheering and Maisy's voice was hoarse and warm. And as she sang there was laughter in her eyes again. And it crept into her voice. Into her hands. In the way she stood. The way she opened her mouth. The way she looked at the people. And they all felt it and it showed in their faces and in their eyes and in the smiles on their lips.

'Now dance!' Maisy cried and pulled a handsome young man to her.

Leah smiled from the side of her mouth and hurriedly brushed a tear away.

'She is a good one, that.'

'Yes. A very good one. That Xuma is a fool.'

Leah swung round. She did not know Ma Plank was near her.

'I did not speak to you, old woman.'

Ma Plank smiled.

'I know. You were speaking to yourself but I heard you. And it is true, he is a fool.'

'Eliza is beautiful.'

'I know, but he is a fool.'

'No man is a fool who takes the woman he wants, old woman.'

'But all men are fools who want the women they take.'

'You are foolish, Ma Plank. You cannot go to a man and say "This is the woman for you, love her." A man will love a woman and that will be all.'

'I know, my child. Was it not so with Daddy. . . .'

Leah squeezed the old woman's hand.

'It is ever so,' Ma Plank said and sighed.

An old woman came along and dragged Ma Plank away. Leah stood alone for a while, watching the party. It had started well. It was going to be a good party. And then, later, in a few days' time, she would deal with Dladla, for this was his party. It was to celebrate her discovery of the traitor.

A huge fire burned in the centre of the yard and it was warming up and people were taking off their coats. Leah called a couple of young men and told them to start smaller fires at other points in the yard.

The ground of the yard had been hardened by mixing cement and horse manure into it and stamping it and then polishing it with a stone. Now it was like the floor of a dance hall. The fires would soon have the whole yard warm then everything would be good.

In a far corner of the yard a group of old women looked after the food. Everything was as it should be.

Leah went into the house. Xuma and Eliza were there. They lingered over their food.

122

'So,' Leah said and smiled at them.

Xuma made room for her on the bench but she went to the bench opposite them. She could see that Xuma was happy. And Eliza, too, was happy. And she was different. Leah could see that. There was a new softness in her eyes, it made her more beautiful. And the hardness was gone from her mouth. And she looked weaker. Her body was not so tight and upright. And her hand kept straying to her side and touching some part of Xuma.

Leah nodded to herself. It is ever so with lovers. A woman finds a man and the world is a new place. And the fighting stiffness that was ever in her body, goes. And the hardness of her head stops and she does not think any more with her head but feels with her heart. Yes, it is ever so. And with a man it is so too. His shoulders square and a smile is not far from his lips and there is a new certainty in him. Yes. It has ever been so and it will ever be so when a man and a woman love.

'You are happy now?' Leah asked.

'Yes, Leah!' Eliza said.

Leah's eyes softened and a smile played round her lips.

'Good. Then let us talk. The talk is between you and me, Xuma.'

'That is good,' Xuma said.

'You listen, Eliza, but remember, it is not your talk.'

Eliza nodded and leaned against Xuma. Xuma slipped his arm round her.

Outside the party was warming up. The music was louder and the laughter and cries of people carried into the room. And occasionally Maisy's voice rose above the voices of the others.

'This one is a fool sometimes, Xuma. I know. I have looked after her all the time and I have watched her and I have seen the things she does, so I know. And I tell you she's a fool sometimes, heh?'

'Yes.'

'Sometimes she will be mad. Let her be. It is the madness of the city. If you were another kind of man I would say beat it out of her. But you, too, are a fool, so let her be, is that good talk?'

'It is good.'

'Good. You are a good man, Xuma, and now you will look after her and I will be finished with her. She is your woman now. And if you have trouble come to Leah for I love you and I love her and I will help you. . . . That is all. The indaba with you is finished, Xuma.'

Leah shifted her eyes to Eliza.

'Now it is for you. For you there is only one thing. Tell me, do you love Xuma or is it the madness that sometimes takes you?'

From outside there was a burst of loud and prolonged laughter. It sounded as though Daddy was up to some madness again.

Eliza looked at Leah and there was that in Leah's eyes that made it hard for her to look away.

'I love him,' Eliza said.

'That is good,' Leah said. 'If a woman loves a man she does that which is good for him. And for you I have this present. The things that are in the small room are for you two when you want to begin your home. . . . Now, Xuma, go out there and find Maisy and dance with her. It would be good. Go on!'

Xuma hesitated, then went out.

'He is a good man,' Leah told Eliza.

Eliza nodded and began to clear up. Leah sat watching her. Suddenly Eliza left the things and went on her knees in front of Leah. She buried her head in Leah's lap and clung to Leah.

Xuma found Maisy in the centre of a group of young men. He pushed his way through. Maisy was laughing, her mouth wide open, beautiful white teeth flashing. The young men wanted her to choose one of them as her boy for the night.

'I will dance only with you,' one said.

'I dance well,' another declared.

'I am the strongest,' said a third.

'I will not walk on you,' said another.

'I will take you home,' offered yet another.

Another took her hand and told her how beautiful she was. And all of them Maisy refused with gay laughter and the shake of her head.

'Can I dance with you?' Xuma asked.

Maisy looked at him and stopped laughing. The young men looked at Xuma.

'Yes,' Maisy said and stepped close to him.

The young men cursed their luck and asked each other who the lucky fellow was.

124

Xuma and Maisy danced in silence. Round them were other couples, jostling each other and calling to their friends and neighbours.

Xuma thought of Eliza and smiled. She loved him! She loved him! And her love was as strong and joyful as his.

'She loves me,' he told Maisy.

'I am happy for you,' Maisy said.

'You are a good friend,' he told her.

'You must remember to go to work,' Maisy said.

'I will,' he said.

The music stopped. People went to where the old women sat with the food. The old women doled out chunks of meat and pieces of bread. Xuma and Maisy stood facing each other, there was little they could say to each other. Eliza followed Leah out of the room and slipped her arm through Xuma's.

'Hello, Maisy,' Eliza said happily.

'You look happy,' Maisy said.

'I am happy,' Eliza said and took her arm.

'Xuma must be at work at twelve, remind him,' Maisy said.

Eliza nodded and looked at her watch.

Maisy walked away. The group of young men were waiting for her. They welcomed her joyously.

The music struck up again. Xuma and Eliza danced. Xuma felt good, dancing with Eliza. She was like a feather in his arms. Light and easy and fast. And the music was in their blood and they did not notice the dancing throng around them. They looked into each other's eyes and held each other tight.

The music stopped. Eliza dragged him to a quiet corner of the yard. They sat on some rugs near a fire. Near them were the old people who were watching the dancing. Eliza made him rest his head on her lap. An old woman gave Eliza some food. She fed Xuma, pushing little bits into his mouth and playing with his hair.

And round them people laughed and sang and danced and told stories. But they were alone and happy. Eliza traced patterns on his forehead and traced the outlines on his face. And every time her hand got near his mouth he snapped at it.

And when they had eaten the food Xuma told her about his home and his people and about the things he had done and the

125

things he had wanted to do when he was a young boy. He told her, with a touch of boastfulness, that he had been the strongest of the boys of his village. He told her about his mother who died. And about his old father and about his young brother.

'You will like them, and you will like the place too,' he ended.

'Yes, it is beautiful,' she said. 'We must visit them, heh?'

'We will!' he declared. 'But first we must make a home and make money so that we can take them presents when we go.'

Then she told him about herself. She had not known her parents. They had died when she was very young and Leah had looked after her. And Leah had been good to her and sent her to school. And she told him what school was like and what people did in schools. And she tried to tell him about the madness that took hold of her at times. That madness that made her hate herself because her skin was black and made her hate the white people because their skins were white and made her hate her own people because they did not want the things of the white people. But it was hard to tell of that for the words would not come. It was hard to explain the emptiness in her breast sometimes or the feeling that made her want to kill people. It was hard to give words to these.

So she said simply, 'It is the madness of the city that is in me.'

He told her not to talk about it. So in silence, holding hands, they watched the dancing and the singing and the laughing of the people. And they were happy. For him it was good to have his head resting on her lap. And for her it was good that his head should rest on her lap. And her fingers played with the outlines of his face. And when his teeth caught them, his teeth were gentle with them.

And over and over she told him she loved him. And over and over he told her he loved her. And it was always a new thing that they told each other.

Leah passed them and smiled. It is ever so with lovers, she thought. She remembered how her man had courted her.

Eliza looked at her watch. It was nearly eleven.

'It is time to go,' she said.

But Xuma would not move so she had to force him up.

The music had stopped and the people had formed a ring and were clapping their hands and stamping their feet. This was the dance of Man and Woman. The dance in which the man and the woman go into the centre of the ring and talk with their hands and their bodies but not with their lips.

Xuma remembered the first time he had danced that dance. It was with Maisy on the corner of the street. It was under a street lamp.

'Let us dance,' he said and took Eliza's hand.

Maisy was the singer for the dance. Her voice rose above the stamping feet and clapping hands.

Xuma and Eliza went to the centre of the ring and Xuma called Eliza to him with his hands, but she would not come. There was pain in her refusal and her body trembled and her face was twisted with the pain of refusal.

The women sympathized audibly. The men encouraged Xuma. And above it all rose Maisy's voice. And some of the pain of Eliza's dancing was in her voice.

Xuma called again, with gentle, pleading movement. Eliza moved nearer to him. One step. Two steps. And then she could not move any more. She danced on the same spot, and hard though she tried, she could not move further towards him. Xuma danced away, dejected and unhappy. Suddenly Eliza was free. She could move forward. Pleading with her hands and calling him with a movement of her head. But he could not hear. He was unhappy and depressed.

The men sympathized with him. The women encouraged Eliza to call him louder.

The rhythm of her dance grew louder, more pleading, faster. Round and round she went. Pleading with her hands. Commanding with her head. Ordering with her feet. Round and round. Faster and faster. Still he danced away, an unhappy and dejected man.

The tempo of Eliza's danced slowed down, became soft and quiet.

Maisy's voice grew soft and quiet.

Half shyly, half eagerly, Eliza danced round till she faced him. Then, with much love in every move, she offered herself. She did not plead and she did not command. She just offered. The dejection slipped from him. They danced up to each other, and holding hands, whirled around in a triumphant swing of victorious love.

The dance ended. People roared their approval. Eliza clung to Xuma, breathing heavily.

'We must go,' she gasped.

People patted them on the backs as they went out.

They went to Xuma's room where he changed his clothes. Eliza went round the room and touched everything.

She walked with him to the spot where they had been that first Saturday. The noise of Malay Camp had died down to a distant buzz. The stars were bright and far. They could see the mine dumps in the distance. Dark, shadowy figures, towering up to the sky.

Xuma rememberd the first time he had been on that spot with her. He had tried to kiss her then but she had fought him. It seemed such a long time ago. Then he knew nothing of the mines. Now he was a boss boy and knew very much. Almost everything.

'Remember that first night?' she asked.

'Yes.'

'You did not know me but you wanted to kiss me.'

'You did not let me.'

'I feared you.'

'And now?'

'Now I fear you more because I love you.'

'You must go back now,' he said.

'All right,' she said.

'Be careful.'

He held her close to him for a few minutes, then pushed her away. He walked hurriedly down the little footpath that led in the direction of the road to the mines. He turned once and waved. Eliza watched him till the pale blanket of darkness covered him. Then she turned and slowly made her way back to Malay Camp.

ELEVEN

A bird sang in his brain. Wearily, perhaps, for he was tired. He rolled on to his side but the singing of the bird was still there. It was clear and came from a very long way off. Xuma sighed in his sleep. The bird threatened to wake him up. Might as well listen to it. He listened and the singing bird lulled him back into deep sleep.

He had returned to his room when the pale, colourless sun was high. He had meant to go to Leah's place. He had known it was too early for Eliza to be there. But he had meant to go there and wait for her, so that she should find him there when she returned from school. Great weariness, however, had forced him on to his bed and now a bird sang.

He slept deeply again and the voice of the bird faded into a dream about Eliza and last night and the party.

Working night-shift was different from working during the day. Time moved more slowly and the work was harder. And it was hard to keep awake.

The voice of the bird returned. It came nearer with a weary persistence. Xuma groaned and rolled on to his back. Now there were other noises with the voice of the bird. He tried to shut them out but they would not go. There was the noise of water and of the wind in the leaves and these were forcing his eyes open.

The voice of the bird changed into the voice of a person humming. He opened his eyes and stared up at the ceiling. The light of day was in the room. And it was not as cold as it had been when he came in.

He remembered he had thrown himself on top of his bed clothes. But now the bed clothes were covering him. And his shoes had been removed too.

He turned his head. There was a warm, glowing fire in the centre of the room. And the sound of the wind in the leaves was the frying of the pan on the fire. But there was no one in the room. He had heard humming and now it was gone.

Again he heard the humming. It came from outside. It came closer to the door. The door opened and Eliza entered carrying a loaf of bread and some paper parcels.

She stopped humming and smiled when she saw he was awake. Xuma was startled to see her there and felt foolish for being startled. He had not expected her to come to the room and make a fire and cook food. Maybe Maisy would do that – but Eliza; he had never thought so.

She put the things she carried on the little table, looked at the frying pan, then went and sat on the edge of his bed. The old iron bedstead groaned. She kissed him lightly.

'Was your sleep good?'

He nodded. It was hard to believe that this one who came to his room and cooked his food and made his room look nice was the same Eliza he had known in the past. Her eyes shone with the same laughter that was in Maisy's eyes. And there was a softness and warmth in them when she looked at him.

'You are not happy to see me,' she said.

'I am. I am! It is just – I did not think. . . .'

She laughed and it was like many bells.

'You did not think I would come and work for you, heh?'

Xuma took her hand and looked at it.

'Yes,' he said.

'You are a fool sometimes. Xuma.'

She hugged him then went to the frying pan and turned the steak. The water boiled. She made tea. She cut bread.

'One would think,' she said, looking at him over her shoulder, 'one would think it is the first time that you love someone.'

'Maybe it is.'

'That is not true.'

Her eyes told him she wanted it to be true.

'Maybe it is,' he said.

'You have not known another woman?'

Xuma stared up at the ceiling and smiled.

'I have known other women but I have not loved them.'

'Many?' Her voice was quiet and formal.

'Maybe two, maybe three.'

'Were they beautiful?'

'I cannot remember.'

'You will say the same when you are tired of me.'

'No. You I love.'

'I have known only one man,' she said.

Xuma nodded. Ma Plank had told him.

'Did you love him?'

'Yes. But not like I love you. Then I was young. Now I am a grown person, and the love of a child and the love of a grown person are two loves.'

Xuma looked at her and laughed.

'What is it?'

'You are not old.'

'I am not a child. . . . Come, we will eat.'

'What is the time?'

'It is nearly six.'

Xuma whistled and jumped up. He had not known it was so late.

'I slept a long time. Why did you not wake me?'

'You were tired. It was good for you to sleep.'

Xuma sat on a low little bench. Eliza sat on the floor, using his knee as an arm rest. Every now and then she looked up from her food and smiled at him.

They sat thus, talking very little and eating and being happy. Xuma found it hard to believe that Eliza was really his woman. She was so beautiful and she was a teacher, but she loved him. She was leaning on him. She had prepared food for him. She had made his room look nice. That was how a woman behaved when she loved a man.

'Those women you have known,' Eliza said, 'were they good?'

'You are jealous,' Xuma said and laughed.

'I am not! You can go out with Maisy and I won't be jealous and I know Maisy loves you.'

'Maisy is good.'

'Yes. . . .'

She took his empty plate and put it aside. She took his hand and looked into the fire.

'Xuma.'

'Heh?'

'Do you want me to come and live here?'

'Yes.'

'Why did you not ask me?'

'I thought maybe you did not want to come. It is only one room. I thought maybe later on we can take two.'

'And if I did not want to come?'

'I did not ask you.'

'Ask me now.'

Eliza looked at him and waited.

He tried to ask her but the words would not come. They were like hard lumps in his throat. He opened his mouth but still no words came. He looked at Eliza and shook his head.

A tender smile broke on Eliza's face. Her eyes lingered on his face for a minute, tenderly, caressingly, then she stared into the fire, holding his big hard hand between her two small soft ones.

They sat like that for a long time. And there was silence around them, and peace. Occasionally the fire crackled. Occasionally a sound floated in from the street. But these were far away, unreal things. Only the silence and the peace were real. Only the two of them sitting there, staring into the fire. Being silent. Only love was real, and two people in love.

The sky darkened and slowly night drew near. People hurried home from work to sit in front of their fires with their men and women. Others hurried from home. To their work. Others had no homes, no loved ones, no work. Some died. Some were born. Some had food. Others went hungry.

The room darkened and the glow of the fire cast shadows in the corners. Xuma and Eliza sat close together, staring into the red, glowing fire. The kettle sang. Eliza looked up at Xuma. He leaned towards her and brushed her lips with his.

'It is good and peaceful to be loved by you,' she said and got up.

While she washed up she hummed, and there was gaiety and lightness in her voice. And there was the flow of dancing in her movements. They were easy and free and happy. She was beautiful and love made her even more so. Made her soft and gentle and full of laughter and music. And every time she passed near him,

132

she somehow managed to touch him. With her dress, with her arm, her fingers on his hair, her leg brushing against his knee.

Xuma watched her. It was good to have a woman around. And she loved him and was happy with him. The madness had gone out of her and she was just a woman, like any woman, only more beautiful, and he loved her and was proud of her.

She made him help her with little things. Putting things in their right places. And the bare little room with nothing on the floor and only an iron bedstead in one corner and a small table in another, was like a beautiful and comfortable home.

Xuma lighted the oil lamp and hung it in the centre of the room.

'We will make it beautiful,' Eliza said, looking round the room.

'Yes,' Xuma said. 'And later we will have two rooms, heh?'

She nodded vigorously and skipped round the room.

Ma Plank stepped silently into the room and shut the door. Neither of them had seen her. They stood near the fire, holding hands.

'Can I come in?' Ma Plank asked gruffly.

Eliza hurried forward and dragged the old woman to the fire. Ma Plank was shivering with cold and her face looked pinched. Eliza gave her a hot mug of coffee.

'I cannot stay long,' Ma Plank said. 'There is trouble and Leah wants you to come now, Xuma.'

'What is it?' Eliza asked.

'They found Dladla,' Ma Plank said.

'Dladla?' Xuma looked at Eliza.

'The police found him,' Ma Plank went on, 'under a hedge near the coloured school. A knife-hole in his back.'

'Dead?' Xuma asked.

'Dead,' Ma Plank said.

'We must go quickly,' Xuma said and put on his coat.

Leah stood in the centre of the room, arms akimbo. Her eyes travelled round the people sitting in various positions round the room. Ma Plank sat with her hands in her lap. Daddy leaned against Ma Plank, his mouth half-open, a drunken film over his eyes. Maisy sat alone near the door. Xuma and Eliza sat close to each other near the door leading to the front of the house.

'Someone killed Dladla,' Leah said. 'I want to know if it was one of you. I must know, for then I will know how to act. Do not hide and do not lie. The police will be here soon. They will come here, for Dladla was betraying me.'

Again her eyes travelled round the room. They rested on Daddy, a long, lingering look. Daddy loved her. Only she knew how much.

'Did you do it, Daddy?'

Daddy grimaced and spat.

'I wish I did,' he said.

Leah looked at Ma Plank.

'No!' Ma Plank said harshly.

'Maisy?'

'I did not, Leah.'

Leah looked at Eliza. She knew Eliza did not do it.

'Eliza?'

'No.'

She looked at Xuma. He might have. But he was with Eliza till he had to go to work. And if he had done it she would have read it in his face. It was like a book, his face.

'Xuma?'

'No. . . . And you?'

Leah smiled a twisted smile from the side of her mouth.

'I did not kill him,' she said.

'Maybe Johannes did it,' Xuma said.

Leah shook her head. 'No. I spoke to him this morning. He did not. Johannes is like you. You can read it in his face.'

'Then who did it?' Xuma asked.

Leah shrugged and turned away.

A motor car drew up outside. White men from the C.I.D. in plain clothes got out. They banged on the door.

'That's the police,' Leah said without turning her head. 'Let them in, Ma Plank.'

Again there was the banging on the door.

'Shut up!' Ma Plank shouted. 'I am coming!'

She hurried to the front door.

Leah stared out of the window into the yard. She looked proud and unbending, a strong, tall woman.

Maisy kept looking at Xuma and then lowering her eyes.

Eliza sat very close to Xuma.

Xuma looked at Leah's back and marvelled. She was the same as ever. Only stronger and more aloof and with more pride in the carriage of her head.

The policemen came through.

'Hello, Leah,' the foremost one said.

Leah turned and looked at him. The ghost of a friendly smile played on her lips.

'You look well,' he said.

He knew Leah well. He had tried to trap her many times. He knew she was one of the foremost Skokiaan Queens – for that is what they call the women who deal in illicit liquor.

'You look well too,' she said. 'What do you want?'

'You know Dladla is dead,' the policeman said.

'I have heard.'

'Who did it?'

'I have not heard.'

'You know he was informing us on you?'

'I have been told.'

'And you did not kill him for that?'

'No.'

'Did you pay someone to do it?'

'No.'

'He betrayed your man and his brother. Did you know?'

'I was told.'

'Who told you?'

'A friend.'

'What's his name?' the man shouted suddenly.

Leah smiled, 'I am not a child.'

The man returned her smile and there was an apology in his eyes.

He looked at Xuma.

'Does he work for you?' he asked Leah.

'He works on the mines,' Leah said.

The policeman looked round the room, studying the faces of the people, then he shrugged and smiled.

'All right, Leah, come with us.'

Xuma jumped up.

'I will go with you, Leah.'

Leah shook her head and smiled at him.

'No, Xuma, stay here and look after these others. I can look after myself.'

Her fingers dug into his arm for a minute, then relaxed.

Suddenly Eliza jumped up. She trembled. Her hands clenched and unclenched. Her eyes blazed and her teeth chattered with anger.

'Get out!' she shouted and rushed at the foremost policeman.

The policeman caught her arms and held her away from him.

'Take her,' Leah said to Xuma.

Xuma pulled her away from the policeman.

'She has done nothing!' Eliza shouted. 'Leave her alone!'

Xuma tried to quieten her down.

'She's wild, that one, heh, Xuma?' the policeman said.

'What is it to you?' Xuma said with flashing eyes.

The policeman smiled.

'They are young,' Leah told the policeman. 'Let them be.'

He stepped aside and Leah went out. He watched her with admiring eyes. Leah's lips were firmly compressed and there was a hardness in her eyes. Her head was held high and her shoulders pushed back as she got into the car.

The crowd that had gathered round the car watched in silence. The foremost policeman – he was nicknamed The Fox by the people of Malay Camp and Vrededorp – got in beside her. The others went in front.

The Fox was liked by the people for he did not behave as a white man. He did not mind sitting beside black people, or even drinking their beer when he was not trying to catch them. And he was feared more than any other policeman for The Fox trapped more people than any other policeman. . . .

Eliza broke away from Xuma and ran out. The car moved off.

'Leah!' Eliza cried piteously. 'Leah! Come back!'

But the car gathered speed.

Eliza stopped. Tears flowed from her cheeks. She bunched her hands into tight little fists. And long and bitter curses against the white man flowed from her mouth.

Xuma had to carry her into the house, still cursing and crying. The car had gone, and Leah with it, and slowly the people dispersed and went about their own business.

Xuma laid Eliza on Leah's bed and stood over her while her body shook with painful sobs. There was nothing he could say to her. All he could do was stand there over her and watch her.

'Maybe Leah will come back,' he said and felt hopeless.

There was nothing one could do. The white man came and said 'Come' and you had to go. And those who remained behind could only watch. They could do nothing. It was hopeless. . . .

Gradually Eliza's sobbing died down till she lay spent and panting. Xuma took her hand and rubbed it. It was cold.

'You are cold,' he said. 'Come, let us go by the fire.'

'Go. I will come soon,' she said.

'I will wait for you,' he said.

'No. You go.'

He went out of the room.

Ma Plank had warmed some coffee.

'I will take some in for her,' Ma Plank said.

She stayed a long time in the room with Eliza.

Xuma and Maisy sat by the fire, not saying a word.

In a corner Daddy wept quietly. Soon he fell asleep.

Ma Plank and Eliza came out of Leah's room. Eliza had wiped her eyes. She went to Xuma and sat near him with her hand resting on his knee. Ma Plank went to Daddy and twisted him so that his neck was more comfortable, then she, too, took a seat near the fire.

They sat in silence. The fire went out. The ashes glowed dully. Ma Plank took it out and brought the other one in that was just ready. They did not speak. There was no life in the place without Leah.

An hour went by.

Another and yet another.

They were all startled by a knock on the front door. Maybe it was Leah. Maybe they had let her go. Ma Plank, Maisy and Eliza rushed to the door in a body. But it was only a neighbour who wanted to know if she could help.

They returned to their seats and the place seemed more depressing.

Another hour went by.

Xuma looked at the kitchen window. His body stiffened. There was Leah, smiling and looking in through the window.

137

'Leah!' he shouted and pointed.

Ma Plank pulled her in and fussed round her, gave her coffee, offered her food, laughed and cried all at once. Leah smiled and hugged the old woman.

Maisy took Leah's hand and kept caressing it. Daddy woke, saw Leah and burst into tears. Then he went to sleep again.

Eliza burst out crying and clung to Xuma, burying her head on his shoulder.

They fussed about Leah as though she had been on a long journey and had not been with them for a long time.

Leah took Xuma's hand and smiled into his eyes.

The neighbours came to greet Leah and to tell her how pleased they were that she had returned.

Everyone treated her as though she had returned from a long journey. People danced outside the house and soon it developed into a party celebration.

Leah took Xuma aside in the midst of all this and said:

'I wonder who killed Dladla.'

'Yes, I wonder,' Xuma said.

But it was never discovered who killed Dladla.

TWELVE

Twilight gathered fast. Xuma and Eliza strolled home through the gathering dusk. It had been so now for five days. They had loved and had been together all the time. And it had been good.

Always, when the work was over, Xuma would come home and go to sleep, and always, as it had been on that first day when he had been awakened by her presence and the cooking and the humming, there would be the singing bird to wake him. And it would be Eliza's voice and she would be preparing food.

And sometimes, after food, they would walk where it was quiet and there was no crowd. They would talk little then, for there was not much to be said. They would just walk. Close together, away from the crowds, where the earth was still and where a slight breeze could touch their faces, there they would walk. They would look at the moon and at the stars, and they would look at the distant, hazy mine dumps, and then they would go back to the room and sit by the fire till it was time for Xuma to return to work. Then Eliza would go with him to the point where they had been that first night together and where they now went often, and there he would leave her and stride away briskly. She would watch him, then. Watch him till the blanket of darkness covered him. Then she would return to the room and there she would sleep. For it was good to sleep in the bed of your man, even when he was not there to sleep with you.

At other times they would go to Leah's after food and they would talk and help with the selling. For now that Dladla was dead there was no one to betray Leah and it was safe to sell. And Leah always said selling meant money, and money meant power.

And then again at other times they would join the crowd and

dance with the crowd on street corners. For that, too, was good when they did it together. Life was good and love was a wonderful thing.

Sometimes Xuma noticed that Eliza was quiet and far away, deep in her own brooding thoughts. His instinct told him when this happened. And when it was so he would go out and walk about for half an hour. And when he returned Eliza was all right again. And after such times she was always sweet and made him love her. And then the passion in her would be strong. And Xuma would marvel at such a small body having so much passion.

Sometimes, at Leah's place, they met Maisy. And with Maisy the old laughter was always there in her eyes and on her lips. It made Xuma wonder whether he had not been dreaming when he had thought Maisy wanted him. Only sometimes, when he was not looking, Maisy would look at him, searchingly, and her eyes would be strange and without laughter. But Xuma did not know that.

For Xuma life was good. He thought of it and of the five days that Eliza had been with him and of the goodness of her love and he smiled happily as they walked home in the gathering twilight. . . .

'You smile,' Eliza said, without looking at him.

'Yes, life is good. It is good to be with you. It makes me happy so that I cannot tell you in words.'

'That is good,' Eliza said.

'You are unhappy,' he said.

'No.'

'It is there in your voice.'

'No.'

'It is there.'

'When will your night-shift finish?'

'Why are you unhappy?'

'Don't be a fool, Xuma. Tell me about your night-shift. It is not good for a woman to sleep alone every night. Go on! Tell me.'

Xuma smiled. 'Another two weeks.'

'Then no more night-shift.'

'No more night-shift.'

'For how long?'

'I do not know.'

They lapsed into silence. They turned a corner. They were near

140

the room. The woman who lived in the room opposite was on the verandah. She waved when she saw them.

'She wants us,' Xuma said.

They quickened their pace.

'What is it?' Xuma asked.

'There was an old woman here,' the woman said. 'She said to tell you Ma Plank has been and you must both go to Leah's quickly.'

'What is wrong?' Eliza asked.

The woman shook her head. 'She did not say. But her eyes were wet and it looks like trouble.'

'Maybe they've arrested Leah,' Xuma said.

'Come on,' Eliza said.

They hurried down the street.

When they got there Ma Plank let them in.

'Is it Leah?' Eliza asked. 'Have they arrested her?'

'No,' Ma Plank shook her head, 'it is Daddy.'

'What is it?' Xuma asked.

Ma Plank bit her lower lip and looked away. Tears streamed down her face. Eliza put her arm round the old woman.

'A motor car knocked him down.'

The old woman could not keep her feelings in check any longer. She cried till the strength went out of her body. Eliza led her to a chair and comforted her.

Xuma went into Leah's room. Daddy lay groaning on the bed. Leah sat on the edge of the bed with Daddy's head on her lap. At the foot of the bed stood Dr Mini whom Xuma had helped with the man who had jumped from the roof and broken his arm.

The doctor recognized Xuma and greeted him with his eyes. Leah turned her head and looked at Xuma with unseeing eyes. Xuma went round the bed and looked at Daddy. He looked as he had always looked, only there was a small bubble of blood on his lips. There was no mark anywhere on Daddy. Xuma looked at the doctor..

'How is he?'

The doctor compressed his lips, shook his head and gave a slight shrug. His movement said, 'He is finished.'

'But you are a doctor,' Xuma said.

'He is damaged inside,' the doctor said.

Daddy groaned. Leah stroked his forehead and murmured soothing things to him as one murmurs to a child. Xuma put his hand on Leah's shoulder. She pulled away.

'There is nothing any one can do,' the doctor said and picked up his bag.

Eliza came in. Her mouth trembled but her eyes were hard and bright and her hands were bunched into hard little fists. She went to Leah. They looked at each other for a little while and it seemed that they spoke without speech.

Daddy opened his eyes. The drunken film had gone from them. They were clear, kind, understanding eyes. He tried to speak but blood choked him. Leah wiped the blood from his lips.

'Go,' Leah said, raising her eyes to the doctor.

The doctor touched her lightly on the shoulder then went out.

Daddy closed his eyes.

Maisy opened the door and came in. She went to Leah. And as it was with Eliza, so Maisy and Leah looked at each other and spoke without speaking.

Daddy coughed and more blood appeared. Leah wiped it away. Daddy opened his eyes again. Xuma was startled by the bright clearness of his eyes. It was as though he was looking at another man. A man he had never known before. Even the face was different. It was the face of a man. A good and kind man. Not the face of a drunken old thing.

'Get Ma Plank,' Leah said, without looking up.

Xuma went out and brought Ma Plank in. Daddy looked at Ma Plank and it seemed that he smiled but his face did not move. Ma Plank smiled and patted his forehead and there was great warmth and love and understanding in her eyes. Daddy lifted his hand. Leah helped him. He brought it down on Ma Plank's hand on his forehead. Daddy closed his eyes and they stayed like that for some time. Then he opened his eyes and now the smile was really on his lips. His eyes were watery and clear at the same time. It seemed as though there was no more pain in him. His eyes lingered on Maisy then and they went to Eliza and lingered there for a while and then he looked at Xuma. It seemed to Xuma that the eyes laughed kindly at him and said, 'So you are Xuma from the north, heh? I am sorry you have not seen me as I am, but there it is and you will not understand.' A lump rose in Xuma's throat.

Then Daddy looked at Ma Plank. She smiled as though she were very happy. It made her face look like the face of a young woman.

And all the time Leah sat there quiet, nursing his head on her lap, looking only at Daddy, her lips firmly compressed and dark, resigned pain in her eyes. And at the same time looking stronger and prouder and more rock-like than ever. Leah. Strong Leah.

Daddy opened his mouth. Ma Plank brought her ear very close to his mouth.

'I am sorry,' he murmured.

'What fool nonsense is this?' said Ma Plank and her voice was light and happy, like the voice of a young girl in love. 'What fool nonsense! Have we not been happy together! Have you not been a good old man to me! Then stop this fool nonsense!'

Daddy smiled and there was happiness in his eyes. He closed them. When he opened them again he looked at Leah. They looked at each other for a long time, Daddy and Leah. Looked at each other with deep understanding that wanted no words. Then Daddy sighed and closed his eyes.

And quite suddenly Daddy who had been drunk ever since Xuma had known him, Daddy who made a fool of himself every day and yet whom Leah respected as she respected no one else, Daddy who loved fighting if others did it, quite suddenly that Daddy was there no longer. Xuma looked at an empty shell. Death shook him.

Silently Ma Plank slipped to her knees. Maisy cried out once and was quiet. Eliza went to Xuma and clung to his arm. Only Leah remained the same. She sat as she had sat while Daddy was alive, nursing his head on her lap, rock-like and distant.

'Leave us,' Leah said.

Xuma, Maisy and Eliza went out.

The two women who had known and loved Daddy before he was a drunken old man, stayed with him.

The lights went out in Vrededorp and Malay Camp. People went to sleep. The streets were quiet when Xuma set out for work, alone. Eliza did not go part of the way with him. . . .

When he came from work the next morning he went straight

there. Leah was as he had left her the night before. Still nursing the empty shell that had been Daddy.

Maisy and Eliza had not gone to work. Between them they had arranged for the funeral. The whole street had helped. The place was full of people. The street had known Daddy and loved Daddy. Some of the older folk remembered Daddy when he had been young and was a man such as Ma Plank had never known. They spoke warmly and lovingly of him. They filed into the room to look at Daddy for the last time. Then they passed out and others filed in. Hundreds of them.

Alone, Leah and Ma Plank washed and dressed Daddy. It was only when he was in the coffin that they allowed others to come near him.

All the time Leah was silent and distant. She spoke only to Ma Plank. Not once did she cry. Not once did a tear drop from her eyes.

The spring sun was high when they buried Daddy in the native cemetery on the hill beyond Vrededorp.

Lena, Johannes' woman who had come out of jail that day, cried all the time.

At the head of Daddy's grave they put a little cross with a number. And under the number they wrote his name. Daddy was called Francis Ndabula. . . .

For a time the people would mourn Daddy, and then they would forget him and the mention of his name would grow rare. Another old man would ultimately become the drunk old man of the street. Maybe they would call him Daddy too. And the Daddy who was Francis Ndabula would be forgotten. Only those of his own house would remember him. And even for them the memory would grow faint and misty. Life is so. . . .

Leah got drunk that night. Really drunk. It was the first time Xuma had seen her so. And she laughed all the time. She would throw her head back, plant her feet firmly and slightly apart on the solid earth, put her hands on her hips and laugh. She did it many times. A deep, joyous well of laughter that shook her body.

It angered Eliza and she would not talk to Leah. But Maisy was kind to Leah. She treated her like a little child. She told Leah what to do and Leah did it. Once Xuma watched her looking at Leah and nodding her head. And Xuma heard her say:

144

'Poor Leah.'

But Leah was drunk and happy. She invited everybody and drinks were free. Beer flowed. But those who talked about Daddy were chased away and for them there was no free beer, nor could they buy any from Leah's place that night.

Suddenly Leah went among the people and raised her hands.

'Quiet!' she shouted. 'Quiet!'

The people quietened down and all heads were turned to her.

'We will dance!' Leah shouted.

She saw Xuma and beckoned to him. He went to her. She clung to his lapel and leaned heavily against him. She smiled sweetly into his face.

'You will dance with me,' she said.

Eliza touched Xuma's arm. He turned to her.

'I will go to the room,' she said.

Xuma nodded.

'I will go with her,' Ma Plank said.

'Let them go!' Leah cried. 'Let them go!'

She glared balefully at them. 'Do you think your tears and black cloth will do anything! Do you think if you tried to hold yourself stiff and hard and look for other people's pity it will help! Fools! What is finished is finished! Teacher, bah! You are the bigger fool! Tears! Tears! Get out before I get angry and kill you both! Get out! Get out! Both of you, get out!' She shouted and there was a wild sob in her voice.

'Go on, Leah, dance,' Maisy said softly.

Eliza and Ma Plank went out. Xuma wanted to follow Eliza, but he knew he had to stay with Leah. He looked at Maisy.

'We must stay with her,' Maisy whispered. 'Ma Plank will come back soon. It is only for a short while that her heart has conquered her head.'

'Come, Xuma, we will dance,' Leah said.

The people formed a ring. Xuma watched Leah, waiting to see what she would do. Leah bowed to him. The people clapped. Then Leah began to whirl round and round. Round and round she went, faster and faster. It seemed as though she could not stop, as though something was forcing her to whirl faster and faster.

And then suddenly she stopped. She rocked from side to side for a little while. Xuma saw that she was going to fall. He hurried forward to catch her but was too late. She fell with a heavy thud and lay in a heap on the ground. Maisy jumped into the ring, motioned to Xuma and began to sing and dance.

Xuma lifted Leah and carried her into the house. The people thought it was part of the dance.

Xuma carried Leah to her room and laid her on the bed. Maisy came in a little later with a wet cloth. She bathed Leah's head. Leah opened her eyes and smiled at them, a sad, crooked smile, then she closed her eyes.

'It is all right,' Maisy said to Xuma. 'You can go now. She will be all right now.' Maisy touched his arm and smiled up at him. 'You have been good. Now go.'

He went out.

On the way to his room he met Ma Plank coming back.

'Is she all right?' Ma Plank asked.

Xuma nodded.

'She loved him,' Ma Plank said simply and went on down the street leaving Xuma looking after her.

She was an old woman, and it showed in her walk. A weary and tired old woman who was a little sick of this business called life.

Xuma turned and went on. He was angry with Eliza. Why had she been such a hard one? Why could she not understand the things that affected a person's life. She had wanted him to go home with her when Leah needed him. She had not understood what was happening. Only Maisy had understood and stayed.

And being angry with Eliza made him strangely sad, made his heart heavy. It made him feel a deep emptiness inside him and he longed to be away from the city. Away from this place where people hid their feelings and their pains in drink, and where others did not understand when one was sad.

He wanted to be away from it all. To lie on green grass and look up at the sky. He wished he had never known Daddy, for the death of Daddy had saddened him even more than the death of his mother had saddened him. With her it was clear and one could understand. With Daddy it was not so. There had been too many strange things. Things that he could not understand properly. Things that made him feel his way like a blind one. And that was no good.

He walked past his room, up the street and stopped at the

corner. He stood there, watching the street, and the people moving up and down. Watching three little children playing in the gutter. Watching a drunken coloured woman trying to get home and using the sides of the houses to help her move. Watching three young men, their caps low over the eyes, smoking opium and looking up and down the street to see if any policeman was in sight.

He did not see Eliza on the verandah. He did not see her come up the street slowly, looking at him. He was not aware of her until she called his name softly. Then he jerked his head round suddenly.

She slipped her arm through his and trembled.

'You are cold,' he said.

She shook her head and made him feel the warmth of her hands. He sensed something strange about her. Something new that he could not put a name to. She seemed more upright, stronger, more like Leah. Yet when he looked at her she was the same. The same beautiful Eliza. He forgot that he was angry with her. There was that in her eyes that made it impossible for him to be angry.

'Do not be angry with me,' she said.

In his mind he said 'What you did to Leah was wrong' but it was only in his mind. With his lips he said:

'I am not angry.'

'That is good. Tonight I want us to be happy, heh?'

She begged him with her eyes. She was truly strange. He had never seen her thus. He nodded vigorously.

'We will be happy,' he said and thought of Daddy.

'Come. We will walk,' she said.

They strolled up the street, away from Malay Camp, away from Vrededorp, into the heart of the city and past even that. And they did not speak. Eliza directed the way. They went where Xuma had never been. The city was behind them now, and Malay Camp lay far to the left. Vrededorp they could not even see.

The streets grew broader and there were no people on them. On the side-walk was beautifully tended grass. And trees grew on the side-walk. The houses had big bay windows and through the windows they could see white people eating and drinking. And they could hear music floating out and the happy laughter of the white people.

It was early, not yet eight, so Xuma did not mind. He had not slept at all since he returned from work but he knew he would not sleep so he allowed Eliza to lead the way.

They passed the houses and climbed a little hill. All this time they had not spoken to each other. He felt that Eliza was with him, and at the same time she was not. There was that strangeness on her. They reached the top of the hill and Eliza sighed.

'Do not look back!' she said urgently.

He followed her on to a flat stone, not looking back. He stood beside her on the stone.

'Now!' she said and turned suddenly.

A cry came from her lips. Xuma turned and looked. He gasped, for below him lay the city, Malay Camp, Vrededorp, the mine dumps – everything. And it was strange to see it like that, as though he were above it, bigger than it. He knew it was all there but he didn't know quite where. The heart of the city he knew, anyone could see that. The lights flashing on and off in green and blue and yellow. The lights making houses in the sky. That was the heart of the city, even a fool knew that. He knew Malay Camp was somewhere to the right now, but where?

'Where is Malay Camp?'

Eliza pointed with her finger. 'That light there, see it. No. The blue one. Yes. Now to the left of it. Can you see the dark spot with only a few lights. That is Malay Camp. From there to where the bridge is. On the other side of the bridge, through the subway, is Vrededorp.'

'From here it is so small,' Xuma said and marvelled. 'When you are there it is big. When I first came to the city I got lost in Malay Camp. I walked there from the afternoon till it was very late in the night. If Leah was not outside her gate I would have been lost. And now it is so small. Just like a big farm.'

'That is the city,' Eliza said dreamily. 'The city.'

Yes, it was all there in a shallow valley. And it looked unreal in the moonlight and the twinkling lights it gave off. It looked like a big, beautiful toy.

'And in it people live,' Xuma said.

Eliza stared down intently. Time and again her eyes swept it from horizon to horizon. And there was a touch of hunger and loneliness in her stare. It was intense when she looked at the long winding road that climbed over the far hill and disappeared behind the horizon. It looked like a thin white line from up here. A toy road leading away from a toy city.

'You were born in the city?' Xuma asked.

'Yes. I was born in the city.'

Her voice was sad. He put his arm round her.

'Show me where,' he said eagerly.

She smiled and rubbed his hand against her cheek.

'In the house of Leah,' she said.

'Show me,' he insisted.

She shook her head but playfully pointed her finger. The house was lost in the shadow that was Malay Camp, among the many other houses that were just like it.

A group of thin, individual clouds travelled through the moon. Below, the neon lights in the heart of the city flashed on and off. On. Off. On. Off. Continuously.

Xuma opened his mouth to speak. Eliza lifted her fingers to it and shook her head. He closed his mouth. From the city came a hum. It drifted up lazily and faded in the boundless skies.

They sat still, not speaking a word, hardly moving. They sat for a long time thus.

And when Xuma looked at Eliza again he saw that she was crying, silently.

'What is it?' he asked.

'It is nothing,' she said and smiled through her tears.

He wiped the tears away for her. It was so hard to understand her when she was like this. But she was with him. She did not try to pull away.

'Xuma,' she said very softly.

He looked at her and she saw how hard he tried to understand and pressed his hand.

'Yes?'

'Do not go to work tonight. Stay with me. . . .' Her voice pleaded.

'I must go. I am the boss boy.'

'But only tonight, Xuma. Please.'

'I must go, Eliza. My white man depends on me.'

He wished he could make her understand.

She smiled suddenly, a gay, dazzling smile and nodded.

'I was foolish,' she said. 'You must go.'

He was pleased. She understood. They remained silent again after that.

Minutes went by. Casually she began to play with his hand, with his arm. The movement of her fingers went on and on till he became conscious of them. He became conscious of her warmth. Conscious of the invitation of her fingers. His blood warmed. He took her hands and squeezed them till she gasped with pain.

'You must love me,' she whispered.

'Let us go,' he said.

'No. Here.'

'But . . .'

'No one comes here. I want you here.'

He could not resist her fingers and her eyes and the strange inviting smile of her lips.

And before Xuma carried her away across the highest tip of the highest mountain, Eliza turned her eyes to the city then shut them tight and clung to him. . . .

THIRTEEN

'Eliza! Eliza!' he called sleepily and rolled over.

Work had been hard the previous night for he had had no sleep. And the strained restlessness of it all showed in his sleep. He had tossed and turned and moaned ever since Ma Plank had been in the room. And now he called Eliza and old Ma Plank did not know what to do.

'Eliza!' he called again.

Ma Plank went to the bed and stood looking at him. She put out her hand to touch him and then pulled it back again. He opened his eyes and saw her hovering over him. He smiled.

'Hello.'

'Hello, Xuma.'

He looked round the room. Everything was as it always was. His working clothes had been put away. The fire was in the centre of the room and the food was on it.

'Where is Eliza?'

'She's gone.'

'Will she be long?'

Ma Plank left him suddenly and went to the fire. She looked very old and very tired. Her feet dragged.

Xuma sat up and scratched his head.

'Where did she go, Ma Plank?'

'She went away, Xuma.' The old woman did not look at him.

'Where?' There was a note of impatience in his voice.

With an effort Ma Plank looked at him and kept her eyes on him.

'She went on a long train journey,' Ma Plank said slowly. 'She told me to tell you that she was going on a long train journey and that she will not return. The journey will last for two days and a night.'

Ma Plank paused. Xuma sat staring at her. He opened his mouth once and shut it again without saying a word. Ma Plank spoke again:

'She said she tried but it was no good, Xuma. And she cried a great deal, son, for she loves you truly. . . . It is hard to explain, Xuma, for the things that are in the mind of another person are always hard to understand. But I know Eliza is a good girl and I know she loves only you. She has the same sickness that Daddy had, Xuma, and I loved Daddy, so I know. . . .'

'Be quiet,' Xuma said softly and sat staring in front of him without seeing anything.

The room was suddenly quiet and strange. And the world was so too, an empty and strange place.

Ma Plank kept looking at him. There was no anger in his eyes. There was nothing in them and they kept looking at one place without seeing that place. She did not know what she had expected him to do but she knew she had not expected him to sit there quietly, staring at one place without seeing it.

'I am sorry,' she said softly.

Xuma did not hear her. She got up and dished him a plate of food.

'She asked me to cook for you,' Ma Plank said, but Xuma did not hear her.

She gave him the food. He ate, mechanically, without knowing or caring. Ma Plank had expected him to ask her more questions but there he was, eating and staring and seeing nothing and tasting nothing. People did not behave like that. When they were hurt they did things. They cried or they shouted or they did not eat or they drank or they were angry or their bodies were stiff. They were not just ordinary, as always.

Xuma became aware of the food and put it aside.

'You have not finished,' Ma Plank said.

'Please go,' Xuma said.

Ma Plank was on the verge of protesting, but she looked at him and changed her mind. Slowly she gathered up her shawl and went out.

'She's gone,' Xuma said and looked round the room.

He tried to think but thinking was impossible. Everything was impossible. Eliza had gone and would not return to him. That was all he understood. . . . Eliza had gone. . . .

Afternoon slipped into evening and Xuma remained sitting on the edge of his bed. Time was a stranger to him.

Maisy knocked and entered. He looked up once, blankly. Maisy smiled cheerfully but there was great pain in her eyes.

'You must dress,' she said and found a shirt and a pair of pants for him.

He dressed and sat on the edge of the bed again.

'Will you work tonight?' Maisy asked.

'No.'

It was Saturday and he did not have to go to work till Sunday night. Maisy was sorry. Work would be good. Hard work helps the heart.

'We must go and dance,' she said. 'My friends in Hoopvlei asked me to come and they said I must bring you too. We can go tonight and come back in time for you to go to work tomorrow, heh?'

Xuma shook his head. Maisy chewed her lower lip then laughed suddenly. 'Leah said she would come too, if you came.'

Xuma got up and tightened his belt. Maisy watched him anxiously.

'I do not want to go to your friends,' Xuma said softly. 'I do not want to go anywhere. Please leave me alone, Maisy. Later, maybe, I will go with you again. Now I want to be alone.'

Maisy hesitated then went out. As the door closed behind her he heard her sobbing. It angered him but he soon forgot that. He went back to the bed and sat on the edge of it.

'She's gone,' he said and wondered, in a curiously detached way, how he felt. But there was no feeling to him. Just a heavy emptiness. No pain. Nothing. . . . Nothing. . . . Eliza had gone. . . .

Twenty minutes after Maisy had gone Leah pushed the door open and came in without knocking. She stood in the doorway for a little while, arms akimbo, her head cocked to one side, a smile on the side of her mouth, and looked at him. Then she advanced into the room.

'Hello, Xuma,' she said harshly and loudly. 'I hear a lot of talk and I see old women and young fools crying, heh?'

Xuma looked at her in silence.

'So you cannot speak, heh? Xuma from the north? And why is this? Your woman has left you! Look at you. Bah!'

'Leave me,' Xuma said.

'O sure, I'll leave you. I'm sick of the weaklings who wear pants and pretend that they are men.' Suddenly her voice changed, became softer and more friendly, but the crooked smile remained on her face. 'She has gone, Xuma. That you cannot undo. She has gone because she is sick of this place, sick of us and because she wants things that we cannot give her. Things that she cannot get here. Maybe she will get them, maybe not. But that is how she is, Xuma. You do not know it, but that is why you love her. . . . I told you you are a fool with people, Xuma, such a fool. You think that if you love a woman and she loves you that is all, heh? For some, yes. For others, no. For Maisy, yes. For Eliza, no. By and by when something happens to you maybe you will understand Eliza. . . . Now . . . Go out, Xuma. Go out and walk. Walk for a long time and when you are tired come back.'

She slipped her hands under Xuma's arms and with one heave raised him to his feet. They stood looking at each other. Leah cocked her left eyebrow and the crooked smile on the side of her face broadened.

'And if you are a man,' she said and looked him up and down. '*If* you are a man, you can come to me after your walk and maybe I will take you to bed.'

She laughed harshly at the expression on his face and slapped her thighs. She pushed him out and watched him walk up the street. Then quickly she went into the room and shut the door behind her. She leaned heavily against the door and sighed. Tears glistened in her eyes. She opened her mouth and took a huge gulp of air.

Leah looked round the room slowly. Here Eliza had been happy sometimes. Yes, it had shown on her face and in her eyes and in her voice. It had shown in the way she had taken Xuma's arm sometimes, she had been happy here for a short while.

Leah smiled wistfully. It softened her face, made it tender and beautiful. And her smile was a wholesome, full-mouthed smile, tender and sad. Two big teardrops slipped out of her eyes and rolled unheeded down her cheeks. She went to the little table.

Above it, pinned to the wall, was a faded old snapshot of Eliza. She looked at it for a long time.

'They don't know how I feel,' Leah said softly and took down the snapshot. She slipped it into the folds of her dress and held her hand over it. Her eyes were the eyes of a mother nursing a child.

She went to the door. There she paused and looked at the room again. Then quickly she wiped her tears away, pushed back her shoulders and went out. She walked briskly down the street.

Eliza had gone. . . .

FOURTEEN

Eliza had gone. . . .

It throbbed in Xuma's brain as he walked. It was the only thing that was real. The only thing that lived. All else was dead around him. He did not see the people hurrying past, did not see the excitement of Malay Camp on a Saturday night, did not see life throbbing and surging everywhere. Only one thing stood out in his brain. One real, living, burning thing. Nothing else.

He walked without knowing where he went. And without caring. Only to walk, to keep on walking, like a million brainless, soulless men, only that he desired. To be lost in the rhythm of motion. To be without sight. To be deaf to sound. Only one leg going forward and then the other, only that. Always.

And as he walked the blankness slowly slipped from his mind And after two hours' of walking he was aware of people and things around. He even took an interest in them. He even looked at some of them with a faint curiosity. And he became aware of himself. Became aware, for the first time, of a pain that gripped his heart till it bled. A pain that brought a lump to his throat. He rubbed his eyes and shook his head to steady the throbbing of his brain.

An awful weariness came over him and he was tired of walking. He stopped and tried to find his bearings. I must go back, he thought. He looked around. There was the flat stone. It was familiar to him. But where had he seen it before? Then he remembered. Last night he had loved Eliza on such a stone.

He turned his head suddenly. Yes. This was where they had been last night. There was the city like a toy with many lights. From here they had looked at it last night. She had asked him not to go to work. She had been strange. She had made him love her here. He could almost see her when he looked at the stone. It was as though she was there, looking at him with those soft black eyes and the lovely dimples when she smiled.

They had been here last night and now she was gone.

Xuma turned and hurried away from the place. His heart pounded and his legs ached but he walked fast. Memory was rushing back on him. The blankness was over. The realization that he would not see Eliza again, that she had left him, was very sharp and real. Not dull and numbing. It was there, hurting. And the lump in his throat choked him.

Everything was dazzling and real. The houses, people, the streets, the cars, the lights, the sky, the earth, everything was real and jarring.

Through his brain, slowly, filtered the things they had done together. Walking together. Dancing together. Sitting silent together. Laughing together. Watching people together. Ordinary things that had a halo around them. All that was ended. It was over. Finished with.

Never again would he wake to the singing bird that would change into Eliza humming. Never again would he sit by the fire with her, eating. Never again would she use his leg as an arm rest. Never again would she cook for him or put a button on his shirt. Never again would they be together.

And it hurt with a sharpness that was deadening.

He got to Malay Camp. He was aware, now, of the warmth around him. Winter was going and the streets were the social centres again. People moved up and down. People laughed. Met their friends. Danced on street corners. Again, with the coming of summer, life began to throb in its slow, warm manner in the streets of Malay Camp.

The life around him made Xuma more conscious of his isolation, of his loneliness, of the absence of Eliza and his great need for her.

He pushed through a group of people. A man grabbed Xuma's arm, protesting against him pushing them aside. Xuma shook the man off and continued down the street. The man got angry, cursed and walked after Xuma. The woman with the man ran after him and grabbed his arm.

'Leave him,' she said. 'You can see he's in trouble.'

Xuma went into his room and stood looking around. Already the room was changing. It was not the same place in which they had had their happiness and their food and their silence. It looked drab, unhomelike, cold, in spite of the fire in the centre. He could not stay there. He went out and locked the door behind him.

Slowly he made his way to Leah's place. He did not want to go there but there was nowhere else to go. He knew no one else. Leah and those around her had been his only friends in all the time he had been in the city. The streets he did not want tonight. They reminded him of Eliza. When a man and woman strolled slowly past him it was more than he could bear. So the only place he knew was Leah's.

Ma Plank was outside the gate. She was watching for the police. Inside selling was going on.

'How are you, Xuma?' Ma Plank asked.

'I am all right,' he said heavily.

'Go in. The others are there. Maisy is there too,' Ma Plank said.

He went in. He looked around. The place was crowded with drinking men and women. Over in a corner he saw Leah. She was selling and laughing with the group of men round her.

Leah saw him and called another woman to take her place. She walked over to meet him.

'Hello, Xuma,' she said and her voice was soft and kind.

She pressed his arm. It made him feel better. When Leah had been in his room earlier too it had been better than when the others had been there.

'It is better now,' she said. 'It hurts but the deadness has gone out of you. That is good.'

He nodded. He knew that she understood, that Leah knew people better than anybody he had ever known. She smiled into his eyes.

'Maybe you should drink tonight,' she suggested. 'Drink a lot and maybe it will help you to forget.'

'No,' he said and shook his head.

'Johannes is inside. Go and speak to him. He is not very drunk yet.' She smiled and looked away. 'Later on he will be J. P. Williamson and it will be hard to speak to him.'

'I do not wish to speak to him,' Xuma said.

158

'All right. Come and sit by me while I sell. Later we will go and meet my friend who will tell me what the police are going to do.'

She led him to her corner and made a place for him. He sat to the left and a little behind her and watched her doling out her scales and collecting shillings and two-shilling pieces in return.

Around him buzzed the voices of people. Around him was the movement of people. An endless stream of people. People coming and getting their drinks and making place for others. And there was much laughter among them, and much colourful talk.

Every now and then Leah would turn to him and make some remark and smile at him. And sometimes she would just look at him and then look away again.

Maisy came out of the house and saw him. Her eyes lighted up and her mouth creased into a broad happy smile. She too saw that the deadness had gone out of him. She hurried over to him and patted his shoulder. He looked at her and smiled. She did not say a word. She just patted his shoulder and looked at him and then she went back into the house.

'That is a good one,' Leah said to him above the din.

'I know,' he said listlessly.

'She loves you,' Leah said.

He looked away in silence.

Johannes came out of the house. Lena, his woman, leaned heavily on his arm. Johannes was drunk. He pushed a man out of the way. The man spilled some of his beer. He protested. Johannes grabbed the man's neck in his huge hand and lifted the man into the air. The man croaked and kicked feebly.

'I am J. P. Williamson,' Johannes roared, 'and I'll crush you sonofabitch!'

'Put him down!' Leah roared and smacked Johannes in the face.

A look of innocent pain showed on Johannes' face. He opened his hand and the man flopped to the ground with a thud.

'You hit me, sister Leah,' Johannes cried plaintively. 'You hit me.' He began to cry.

For a moment Leah was amazed by the sight of Johannes in tears. He was so big and tall, so strong that it shocked her to see him cry, and then she burst out laughing. It was so funny.

'You hit me,' Johannes wailed and tears streamed down his face.

His woman, Lena, began to sniff as well, and soon they were both crying.

Leah's sides shook with uncontrollable laughter. Xuma could not help himself, he laughed too. The poor man whom Johannes had dropped was left unheeded on the ground. He lay on the ground looking in amazement on the spectacle of Johannes and his woman in tears.

A man near Leah snickered. Johannes took a step forward, glaring at the man and tears streaming down his face. The snicker died in the man's throat. Leah stepped between him and Johannes. The man looked for a way out. None of the others dared to laugh. Only Leah and Xuma. Maisy came into the yard, saw what was happening and collapsed with laughter. Leah looked at Xuma, saw him laughing and a new note of happiness slipped into her laughter.

Johannes and his woman cried piteously.

'What is this?' Leah asked.

'You hit him,' Lena said and cried all the more.

'You struck me,' Johannes said.

'You choked that man,' Leah said, trying to control her laughter.

Johannes gave the man one contemptuous look and spat.

'He struck me first.'

'That's a lie.'

'Is that not so?' Johannes asked Lena with a violent push.

'Don't push me!' Lena cried and grabbed his arm.

Lena tried to sink her teeth into Johannes' arm but he shook her off as though she were a feather.

'Ask Xuma,' Johannes said. 'He saw the man strike me.'

Leah smiled and looked at Xuma.

'Is that so, Xuma?'

'No.'

'Well, Johannes?'

Johannes hung his head.

'You brute!' Lena said suddenly. 'Apologize to the man. Say you are sorry. Go on!' She rolled up her sleeves and advanced on him.

'Go on, Johannes,' Leah said. 'I will not let you interfere with my customers. Say you are sorry.'

Lena pounced on him. He shook himself and she went spinning. Sheepishly he leaned towards the man on the ground and held out his hand. The man pulled away fearfully.

'Take his hand,' Leah urged. 'He will not strike you.'

Tentatively the man took Johannes' big hand. Johannes pulled the man up.

'I am sorry,' Johannes said.

The man nodded and moved away.

'Sonofabitch,' Johannes muttered under his breath.

'That's good,' Lena said and took Johannes' arm. 'Now you can buy me a drink.'

'Give this sonofabitch a drink,' Johannes said and gave Leah a ten-shilling note.

'I will keep the change for you. You will need it tomorrow.'

And everywhere people ordered their drinks. The place reeked with the smell of beer. The voices of drunken men and women buzzed in conversation. The air was the air of Malay Camp and the other dark places of Johannesburg on a Saturday night. An air that is found nowhere else on earth except in the dark places of Johannesburg.

'Come, Xuma. I am going up the street to meet my friend who will have news for us.'

Xuma followed Leah out. Ma Plank was still out there.

'Everything is clear,' Ma Plank said.

'I am going to find out the plans of the police,' Leah said.

She and Xuma went up the street. Occasionally she looked at Xuma but he was deep in his own brooding thoughts.

'I miss her too,' Leah said.

Xuma looked at her. Of course she loves Eliza too. She had watched Eliza grow up so Eliza must be like a child to her. Of course she loves Eliza too.

'Yes. You love her too,' he said.

'We all love her.'

'And she?'

'She loves you, Xuma. I know. And I'm not a fool with people.'

'But she left me.'

'She left me too. And Ma Plank. . . . And she loved us too.'

They got to the corner of the street and waited.

Five minutes, ten minutes went by. Then they saw the black policeman on the cycle coming down the street. He stopped.

'Hello,' Leah said. 'What is news?'

'I am worried,' the man said. 'They look at one strangely.'

'That is your business,' Leah said gruffly. 'I pay you to tell me what they plan, not how they look at you. What do they plan?'

'You are hard,' the man said.

'Life is hard. What do they plan?'

'They will not come tonight and not in the morning either but in the afternoon tomorrow and tomorrow night they will not leave the place alone for an hour.'

'Good,' Leah said and counted out five one pound notes.

The man pocketed the money and rode off.

'We will not sell at all tomorrow,' Leah said thoughtfully. 'I think that is best. We will take out the tins tonight. What do you say, Xuma?'

'You know about these things,' Xuma said.

They went back to the house in silence. Maisy met them at the door.

'Let us walk, Xuma,' Maisy said.

'Go with her,' Leah said and pushed him.

'All right.'

'But do not stay too long,' Leah said. 'We must take up the tins tonight and you can help. Now go.'

Maisy slipped her arm through his and led him in the direction of Vrededorp. For a long time they walked in silence. Maisy kept turning to the left till they walked where grass was underfoot.

'Where is this?' Xuma asked.

'It's the sports field for the coloured children. This is Fordsburg. It's half-way between Malay Camp and Vrededorp. Let us sit on the grass.'

She pulled him down beside her.

They lay on the lush grass. Xuma, on his back with his hands pillowing his head; Maisy, leaning on one elbow, her body turned to him.

Xuma looked up at the young moon. Pain seemed so ordinary. So much a part of life. He thought of home and the people there and knew that he would never go home again. He did not want to go home. It was no longer home. But at home now, if he were lying

162

in the grass, there would be countless little glows everywhere, the glow of the little fireflies as their lights went on and off all the time. And there would be the quiet without the deep undertone of buzzing that one heard in the city. But home was finished. The going of Eliza had ended it. He had dreamt of going home with her.

'It is quiet here,' Maisy said. 'I like it.'

Xuma thought of the fireflies at home and said nothing.

Maisy looked at him and then looked away. Her eyes picked up a distant, faint, flickering light on the horizon. A light that was weak and could hardly sustain itself. She kept her eyes on it.

'Xuma.'

'Heh?'

'She was a good one.'

He turned his eyes to Maisy and remained quiet.

'Leaving you made her sick, Xuma. And now, tonight, wherever she is, she is lonely and longing for you for she loved you.'

'Do not speak of her.'

'We must speak of her. She is in your brain and it is better to speak of a thing that is in your brain.'

'I do not wish you to speak of her!'

Maisy remained staring at the distant flickering light.

'All right, I will speak of myself for I want to speak. I am tired inside and it will be good for me to speak.' She paused and licked her lips, then she went on in a matter-of-fact-voice, speaking as though she were discussing something of no importance. 'To love a man who loves another is painful. Maybe it is more painful than it is to love someone who loves you and leaves you. I don't know. All I know is it is very painful to love a man who loves another. You look at him and see the light in his eyes for the other woman and your heart bleeds. You lie down to sleep and you are alone and it seems no one wants you and you think "They are together" and it hurts so that sleep will not come. And all the time you carry it in your breast. You look at them when they are together and you smile but inside you bleed. Day after day, all the time it is so. That is pain, Xuma. That is the pain I have carried for months. . . .'

Violently she pulled a tuft of grass out of the ground and flung it away. There was a world of bitterness in it. For a long time there was silence between them after that. She turned her eyes from the distant, flickering light and looked at him. She said, in her quiet, husky, matter-of-fact voice:

'I knew your love would end. I just knew. Eliza is so. She wants things that we do not understand. I waited. Now it is over and I am not happy. Maybe it is because I know now that she really loves you even as you love her. I don't know, maybe it is that. But I am not happy now. I thought I would be happy when she left you and you turned to me. But I am not happy. . . .'

She looked at him for a little longer. And through the darkness Xuma thought he saw the ghost of a smile on her lips. Then suddenly she collapsed, buried her head in her arms, and cried bitterly. Wild, unrestrained sobs shook her body. Pain and torture escaped through her lips. And, mingled with her cries, were words that were muffled by the good earth and the lush, green grass.

Xuma raised himself and looked at her. There was nothing he could do, nothing he could say. He could not even touch her. All he could do was look at her and listen to the pain of her voice. He could not help her.

Far on the horizon the weak light flickered faintly. The young moon was as bright as ever. And the quiet of the night was intensified by the low hum of the city. The stars were in their place. The world was all right.

Gradually Maisy's sobbing died down. The gasping subsided. Her breathing grew even. At last she lay spent and tired, breathing easily and evenly. The storm had shaken her to the core, then it had passed. Now it was over and she lay resting. Time came back, and the world.

Maisy lay still for a long time, eyes closed, her fingers feeling the sharpness of the grass. At length she sat up and wiped her eyes. Xuma lit a cigarette and inhaled deeply.

'We must go back,' Maisy said and stood up.

They walked back slowly, without speaking. Maisy had taken his arm. Maisy was the same as ever.

It was late and the streets were emptying.

When they got to Leah's place the last customers were leaving. Leah was in the yard talking to Ma Plank and the two women who were going to help with the taking out of the tins.

'Here are the children to help us,' Leah said and patted Xuma on the back. 'I will mark the places and you will dig.'

They waited while Leah marked the places. There were five places. Leah gave them each a place and told them how to dig.

'You will watch outside, Ma Plank.'

Ma Plank went to the gate.

Leah fetched little hand spades.

'Now hurry up!' she called and began to dig.

Xuma's tin was the first out. It was half-full of beer. The next was Leah's. Maisy called Xuma to help her lift her tin out. The two women got theirs out. Three tins were empty. One was half-full and one was completely full.

'Now we will take them away,' Leah said.

Suddenly the yard was full of people. People came from everywhere except the gate. Torches flashed. For a split second there was confusion. A torch shone full into Leah's face. Leah stared at the glaring light without blinking her eyes.

'Hello Leah,' a white voice said softly.

'Take the light off me,' Leah said.

The Fox switched off his torch.

'So I've got you at last,' he said.

Leah smiled from the side of her mouth and pushed her shoulders back.

'Yes, you've got me.'

'Let's go into the house, Leah, I want to see you and your friends.'

Leah led the way. The Fox followed her. A policeman brought each of the others along. Two policemen guarded the five tins.

The Fox looked round the faces. He recognized Xuma.

'Hello, Xuma.'

Xuma remained silent. The Fox looked at Leah. There was admiration in his eyes as he saw her composure and the crooked smile on the side of her face.

'I set a trap, Leah, and the mouse jumped into the trap. And what a jump! I've got enough to put you away for six months, Leah.'

'How did you set your trap?' Leah asked.

The Fox smiled, a friendly smile.

'Nobody betrayed you. I knew someone was telling you our plans so we made the wrong plans. We planned not to come tonight but to come tomorrow afternoon. Your friend told you and we made a mistake and came tonight instead. We have been on the roofs for two hours.'

'That was clever,' Leah said.

'I am the Fox.'

Leah nodded.

'There is one thing, Fox. These others were doing what I told them. I want you to leave them. You are a man and if you are my friend you will do it. You wanted me. You've got me. Leave these others.'

'Who brings you the news?' The Fox asked.

Leah shook her head. The Fox smiled and Leah saw the admiration in his eyes. He nodded.

'They can go?'

'Yes Leah, they can go.'

'Thank you. You are a good man.'

'You are a good woman, Leah. Are you ready?'

'Give me a little time.'

'Don't be long. It is late and my wife is waiting for me.'

Leah nodded. She turned to Xuma.

'Call Ma Plank.'

Xuma went out and returned with Ma Plank a few minutes later. The old woman took the whole situation in with one sweeping glance then looked at Leah. Leah smiled and there was a responding flicker in the old woman's eyes. These two realized fully what had happened. The others were too shocked. Leah rested her hand lightly on the old woman's shoulder.

'I shall be gone for about six months, Ma Plank. Sell everything and keep the money. Keep it with the other money. We will need a new home when I return, heh? And remember, don't waste the money on lawyers. Good?'

Ma Plank nodded and went into Leah's room.

Leah looked at Maisy and there was a tender light in her eyes. Leah was the strongest and calmest person in the room. Firm and strong and solid.

'Good-bye Maisy – be a good girl. Look after Ma Plank, she's getting old, and old people want care.'

Maisy's chin trembled. Two tears tumbled out of her eyes, but she smiled. She nodded vigorously.

166

'Well, Xuma from the north,' Leah said, and her voice was light and bantering. 'Well, everything happens together, heh?'

'I will come with you,' Xuma said.

Leah shook her head. 'No Xuma. I go alone. I want to go alone. I am sorry everything happens together. First Daddy then Eliza and now this. Life is so always. I shall worry over you for you are like a big son to me and a son is always dear to the heart of a mother, heh?'

She held out her hand, a big strong capable hand. Xuma took it. He could feel the strength of her grip.

Ma Plank returned from Leah's room with a shawl. She slipped it over Leah's shoulders.

Leah turned to the policeman, her left eyebrow was raised, the twisted smile played on her lips.

'I am ready, Fox.'

The Fox stepped aside. Leah went past him.

'I am sorry,' the Fox whispered.

'You are a fool,' Leah said and laughed defiantly.

Her head was thrown back. Her shoulders were squared. She walked with easy, confident strength. Leah. Strong Leah.

The others watched till the procession turned the corner and was out of sight.

Long after they were gone Xuma still saw the twisted smile on Leah's lips, still heard the defiant laugh that had been the last sound he had heard from her. Eliza had gone. . . . And now Leah was not there.

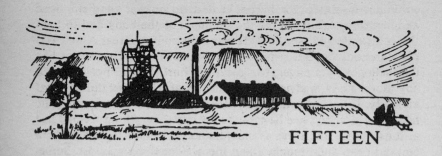

FIFTEEN

Light followed dark and dark followed light. For days it had gone on and on like that. Time had lost its meaning. All things were unreal. And above this unreality was the sky and the earth and people. There was eating and working and sleeping and drinking. People were the same. They quarrelled and they fought and they laughed and they loved. It seemed as though the world did not care about people. And people did not care as well. This big earth that they said was round like a ball, it kept on its own way. Eliza went and it kept on. Daddy died and it kept on. Leah went to jail and it kept on. How is it? Why is it? Who cares about people?

Xuma stopped and lit a cigarette. He flung the matchstick away and looked up at the moon. It was round and big and was fast travelling west. Morning was not far away.

He had just left the mines. He tried to think about his work but his mind kept going back to Leah. He had been in court when she was tried. Leah had stood in the little box where they put all the prisoners. She had smiled at him and her eyes had been calm and friendly. And then the white man had told her she must go to jail for nine months. And they had put her picture in the white man's newspaper. And outside the court there had been a young one who told everybody that white people sold beer and other drinks and didn't go to jail. And he said the only way to stop the Skokiaan Queens is to make bars for black people.

Why is it wrong if Leah sells beer and right if a white person sells beer?

Since that Saturday night when Leah had walked down the street with policemen flanking her, all feeling had left Xuma. Only a tiredness remained. A tiredness and many questions that were a strain on his brain for he could find no answer to them. And sleeping, too, was hard, for the tiredness of the body had to fight the restlessness of the mind. It was as though the real Xuma was dead and only a shell remained. There was feeling, but it was like the feeling of a stranger, for it did not hurt. He did not feel pain any more. There was no lump in his throat. His heart did not beat violently. He could smile easily. He did all the ordinary things he had learned to do since he came to the city. Everything seemed just as it had been. But it was as though another person looked at them and did them and thought about them. Something was lost. Something that had been there all the time, inside him. It was not there now.

Ma Plank and Maisy had come to his room to do things for him. They had tried to cheer him. But he had needed no cheering. He had not been unhappy. It had only been hard to speak to Ma Plank or Maisy, but they had not understood. They had thought he was unhappy.

He had wished they would not come to his room but it had been too much trouble to ask them, so he had left them and they had come. They had tried to speak but there had been nothing to say. Then, after a time, they had stopped coming. The last time Maisy had been to his room she had stood at the door and said, 'When you want me, come to my work place. Ma Plank is there with me. We will be happy to see you.' Then she had gone. Many days ago that had been. . . .

Xuma sucked at his cigarette and watched the speed of the moon. He kicked a clump of earth and sat down.

Strange how everything had changed without Leah. Days had rolled into nights and nights had rolled into days. All dreadfully monotonous and tiring. And he had felt like a stranger in a strange place. He thought of the night he had gone to the house that had been Leah's. He had left his room and walked slowly. And people had greeted him for he had become a citizen of Malay Camp and people showed it in their eyes. And he had known that they knew about Eliza, for in a strange manner that no one knows the people of Vrededorp and Malay Camp get to know about everybody else. Sometimes when he passed them, one person had said to another:

'That is Xuma who works on the mines. His woman left him.

And Strong Leah whom he loves as a child loves a mother, is in jail. And it all happened at the same time.'

It had been thus on that night when he had walked slowly down the street. He had turned left, then right, then left again. And around him had been people.

He had strolled slowly up the street where Leah had lived. The street had been the same. The houses the same. Everything the same. Then he had seen the house. The same house. Almost he had seen Ma Plank standing at the gate, and Leah leaning out on the verandah, and Daddy being drunk in the street. Almost he had seen Eliza standing beside Leah and smiling so that the two dimples showed and her beautiful white teeth flashed. Almost he had heard Maisy's carefree laughter and seen thin, small Lena trying to bully big Johannes. Then suddenly the illusion had faded. A woman had come out and stood on the verandah. She had been short and fat, almost round. Not tall and strong and well-built like Leah. A man who limped slightly, had joined her. He had turned quickly and walked away. It had been painful to see that the house that had been Leah's had become a house of strangers. Strangers lived in it and laughed in it and slept in it and talked in it. It had been painful for the house had meant much to him. It had been the first house in which he had slept when he came to the city. The first house where he had made friends. The house where he had found Eliza. Where Eliza had been born. The house where Daddy and Ma Plank had lived with Leah. *It had been Leah's house.*

Xuma smiled bitterly and picked up a fistful of sand. The big moon was travelling fast and the stars were fading. Day was hurrying along.

He heard the crunch of hobnailed boots on pebbly earth and looked up. A man was coming towards him. It was a big man but he was too far to see clearly. Xuma watched and waited. As the man drew near he saw that it was the Red One.

'Ho there, Zuma!' Paddy called.

Xuma answered and waited. Paddy came up and flopped beside him on the ground. He fished out a packet of cigarettes, took out one and held the packet to Xuma. They lit their cigarettes. Xuma looked at the white man and waited for him to speak. Paddy remained silent, looking up at the sky and watching the moon.

'What is it?' Xuma asked ultimately.

170

'It is hard to say,' Paddy said. 'When a man is sick in the body you say "that and that is wrong with this man" and you go to a doctor and the doctor gives you medicine and says "take this so many times a day and you will get well", heh?'

'Yes?'

'Good. That is so. But now there is this, and maybe you can tell about it. If a man has the sickness of the mind what must he do? He cannot go to a doctor.'

'He must bear it,' Xuma said, looking at the moon.

'That is not the wisdom your forefathers taught.'

'That was before the white man came.'

'And now, after the white man has come?'

'There is nothing to do.'

'Not even to fight?'

'How can you fight guns with bare hands?'

'You misunderstand, Zuma, not that sort of fight. There is another way.'

'What is it?'

'You must find it, Zuma. Out of your feeling and out of your pain it must come. Others have found it. You can too. But first you must think and not be afraid of your thoughts. And if you have questions and you look around you will find those who will answer them. But first you must know what you are going to fight and why and what you want.'

'Why do you, a white man, talk to me like this?'

'Because first, Zuma, I am a man like you, and afterwards I am a white man. I have seen the sickness of your mind. I work with you every day and I saw your sickness and I understood.'

Xuma turned his eyes to Paddy and stared at him.

'You say you understand, white man.'

Paddy nodded.

'You say I must speak what is in my heart?'

Again Paddy nodded.

Xuma looked away and was silent. Paddy waited. The moon was far to the west. The stars could hardly be seen. And the black man and the white were like two men alone in the world. There was no other sign of life around them. In the distance they could see the mine dumps towering against the sky, and in the opposite direction they could see the tall buildings of Johannesburg. There was a hush in the cool morning air. It was as though the world held its breath.

'You say you understand,' Xuma said, 'but how can you? You are a white man. You do not carry a pass. You do not know how it feels to be stopped by a policeman in the street. You go where you like. You do not know how it feels when they say "Get out! White people only." Did your woman leave you because she is mad with wanting the same things the white man has? Did you know Leah? Did you love her? Do you know how it feels to see her go to jail for nine months? Do you know Leah's house? Did Leah take you in in the middle of the night?' Xuma's voice rose. 'Did Leah talk to you and laugh with you from the side of her mouth? You say you understand. Did you *feel* these things like I do? How can you understand, white man! You understand with your head. I understand with pain. With the pain of my heart. That is understanding. The understanding of the heart and the pain of understanding, not just the head and lips. I feel things! You want me to be your friend. How can I be your friend when your people do this to me and my people?'

Xuma got up.

'What you say is true, Zuma, these things have not happened to me so I do not feel them, but tell me this. Do you think a black man can feel them if they did not happen to him? Has Johannes got the same feeling about Leah, about Eliza? He did not love Eliza. Maybe he's sorry for you because you are his friend. But can he feel like you did about Eliza? Tell me.'

'Johannes is black like me and he knows Eliza left me because of the white man, he knows Leah is in jail because of that. When he is sober there is great unhappiness in his heart because he knows these things.'

'There is always great unhappiness in my heart.'

'You are white.'

'I am a man first. I want you to be a man first and then a black man.'

'I am a black man. My people are black. I love them.'

'That is good. It is good to love one's people and not to be ashamed of what one is. But it is not good to think only as a black man or only as a white man. The white people in this country think

172

only as white people and that is why they do this harm to your people.'

'Then I must think as a black man.'

'No. You must think as a man first. You must be a man first and then a black man. And if it is so you will understand as a black man and also as a white man. That is the right way, Zuma. When you understand that you will be a man with freedom inside your breast. It is only those who are free inside who can help free those around them.'

Xuma shook his head and stared away to the east. The first rays of the morning sun were showing against the sky. Bright streaks against the blue. He had told the white man the truth. He had expected the white man to be angry. He had even thought the white man might tell him not to come back to work. But the white man was not angry. And the white man was persistent. He was a good one. A kind one. Xuma looked at Paddy.

'You are kind, Red One, which is good. So many are not kind. So it is good to have people who are kind to us. But it is not kindness that I want.'

'It is not kindness that I offer,' Paddy said and there was anger in his voice. 'I thought you wanted to understand things. Maybe I was wrong. Maybe I should have gone to my bed. Maybe you are just a fool who is afraid to think!'

Paddy jumped up and walked away.

Xuma watched him go. The shadow of a smile touched his lips.

'Sleep well, Red One!' he shouted. And there was friendliness in his voice. He watched till Paddy topped a little hill and disappeared from sight. Then he turned and walked in the direction of Malay Camp.

The Red One's anger had reminded him of Leah. She had spoken to him with that kind of anger and it was strange that a white person should do so too. He thought about Paddy's words. Turned them over. Examined them. To be a man first, think like a man first, and then a black man. How could it be? It would mean people are without colour. But people are not without colour. There are white and black and brown people. All people have colour. Then how can one think of people without colour? But it was a nice thought. Yes. Very nice. No white and no black. Only people. Why, if it were so then he could go anywhere and nobody would stop him for a pass. And then Eliza would have been with him still. If it were so he would get the same money as the Red One. And he would go in the same buses as white folks. But indeed it would be nice! If it were so he would feel a man. . . . Like a man. . . . That is what the Red One said! Like a man! Not a black man and not a white man, just a man. And Leah would not be in jail! If it had been so he would have been on his way to Leah's place now – no, they would be sleeping. No, not to Leah's place. To his room to sleep till Eliza arrived from school and there was a fire in the centre of the room and the frying of meat. . . . And later they would have gone to Leah's place. . . . If it had been so Eliza would have been with him and she would have been happy and without that madness. . . . If only it were so. . . .

He walked through the empty streets and his brain buzzed. Picture after picture slipped through his mind. He felt light and free and gay. People were people. Not white and black people. Just people. Ordinary people. And one could understand a white person as well as a black person. And be sorry for white as well as black. His own secret resentment against all white people disappeared. There were no white people. Only people.

The vision carried him along. He could see himself and Eliza and Paddy and Paddy's woman all sitting at a little table in one of those little tea places in the heart of Johannesburg and drinking tea and laughing and talking. And around them would be other people all happy and without colour. And everywhere in the land it was so. On the farms it was so. People worked side by side and the earth was cheerful and rich and yielded a fat crop and there was food for everybody and work for everybody and there was singing while people worked and there was much laughter. And in the cities too it was so. People worked. People ate. People were happy. And oh the laughter! It was like a huge wave that swept over the land. And all eyes shone with it as they worked in the sun, and there was a new brightness in the sun. . . .

Xuma got to his room and undressed without noticing it. . . . And above all this was man. Man the individual, strong and free and happy, and without colour. Man alive. Pushing out his chest and being proud. Man in his grandeur.

And the country was the good country. And the world was the

174

good world. Full of laughter. Full of friendliness. Full of food.
Full of happiness. The good world. . . .
    Xuma drifted into blissful slumber
    . . . If only it were so. . . .

SIXTEEN

Night had settled over Johannesburg when Xuma woke. His room was in darkness. He rolled over on to his back and reached out for the matches to light his candle. Then he changed his mind and pulled his hand back. He lay still in the dark and felt the emptiness of his belly and the unsteady throb of his heart. The pounding of his heart seemed loud and harsh. He remembered his talk with the Red One. He remembered the beautiful dream with which he had gone to bed. Man without colour and laughter everywhere. It had all been so beautiful and good. But could it be? No. It could not be. How could it be done? But to that there was no answer. The white man will not let it be. So there was no answer.

Reaction set in. He felt alone and bitter and unhappy. The world was a dark place. Darker than it had ever been. Before he had been unhappy and lonely but not like this. Before his unhappiness had been only feeling. Since then he had seen the dream. Man without colour. Now he had something against which to set his pain and unhappiness and it made it greater. It made it too big for him to bear. It pressed in on him and hot waves of pain and hatred rose in his breast and made his eyes burn. Yes! He hated all white people and he hated the Red One. If the Red One had not spoken to him it would not have been so now. But hatred did not ease the tightness round his head. It made it worse. He wanted something that would take that tightness away. To feel as he did before the Red One had spoken to him, just empty and without so much feeling, even that would be better than feeling as he did now. Oh how he hated the Red One!

Then the emptiness of his belly overwhelmed him. He struck a match and lit the candle and got up and dressed. There was bread in the room but it was stale. There was mealie meal and raw meat but he did not want to cook.

He washed his face and went out. There was an eating-house in the next street. He would go there. Sometimes they cooked flies with the meat but no one had yet died of eating their meat. Besides it would be hot and there would be people there. He walked down the street.

Round him people moved, a surging, throbbing crowd. Always it was so. A person would go away, like Eliza; or another would die, like Daddy; another would go to jail, like Leah; but always the crowd would be there. The same crowd of nameless people, moving and living and laughing and fighting. People died, people went away, people went to jail, maybe one or maybe a hundred. But they were people not a crowd. Maybe the crowd never died. Maybe the crowd was the same as it had been since the beginning of time. Maybe crowds never die. And maybe everywhere in the world there are crowds like this, across the waters too. Crowds always going on and on and on. And the same everywhere. And the white ones? Why did he have to think about the white ones. But maybe they were the same too. Yes, maybe.

Xuma got to the eating-house. It was full. He looked round and saw a place where he thought he could squeeze in, far in the corner. He went to it. His shoes grated against the sawdust on the floor. The smell of bad meat hung over the place. A babel of loud voices mingled with the louder din of fat meat flies.

Xuma squeezed himself into position and shouted for food. A dirty ragged old man dumped a plate of meat, swimming in its own gravy, and a hunk of bread, on the dirty table. The old man held out a greasy hand. Xuma pushed a shilling into it.

While he ate he compared the place to the places where white people went. White people did not have to crowd into the place and sit on top of each other. They had bigger rooms. Not just one little room. They had nice eating houses in almost every street of the city.

And again he thought about the beautiful world where man would be without colour. If it were so then all people could eat in nice clean places. And without flies being around you all the time.

Suddenly Xuma felt lonely. He wanted to talk to somebody

about it. Somebody who would understand him. Maybe there was somebody here. He looked at the man sitting next to him. The man looked all right, only his mouth was stuffed full and his eyes were angry as he tried to knock the flies away.

'The white man has good eating-places,' Xuma said.

His voice was drowned by the awful din.

'What?' The man turned his head to Xuma.

'Good eating-places!' Xuma said.

'Too many flies!' the man shouted.

Xuma sighed. He wanted to talk to somebody in a quiet place. To somebody who would understand what he was saying. He got up.

'Going?' the man asked.

Xuma nodded and went out.

Outside, he stood and watched the crowd for a little while. The desire to be with somebody was still strong. It would make him feel better if he could talk to somebody about the things that were going on in his brain. Maybe just putting them into words while somebody listened would help.

Maisy was the person he wanted to talk to. Had he not always felt at peace when he was with her. Yes, he would go and speak to her. He wondered what Maisy had been doing since he last saw her. Maybe she had a new boy friend. Thinking about it worried him. He did not want her to have a new boy friend. Yesterday he would not have minded. But now it was different. Now it would be wrong if she had a new boy friend. He did not know why, but he knew it would be wrong, and he would be very unhappy if it were so.

He set off for Maisy's place of work. And as he drew near the feeling that she might have a new boy friend grew stronger, and his knowledge that it would be wrong also grew. And as he marched his footsteps said, 'It would be wrong. It would be wrong. It would be wrong,' over and over again till his brain buzzed with it. And his anxiety that it should not be so grew apace.

Now he was almost there. It would be good to see Maisy, and also Ma Plank. Would Maisy be glad to see him? Really glad? His clothes were not too clean. Maybe she would not want to see him. Maybe she would not be there.

He dusted the lapels of his jacket with his fingers, tucked his shirt more neatly into his belt and looked with despair at his shoes.

When he got to the gate of Maisy's place of work he was trembling with anxiety. He looked at the gate and licked his lips. He must not show his nervousness. He must be calm. That is manly. And he must tell Maisy he had only dropped in to talk about something that was worrying him a lot. But how was he to tell her about being a man without colour? He tried to think about it but his brain would not work. The words that had been ready on his tongue were there no more.

He turned away and hurried back to Malay Camp. He could not talk to Maisy, and maybe Maisy would not want him to talk to her, and maybe she would not understand him.

It was best that he did not go. He would go back to his room and change into his working clothes and lie on his bed and think till it was time for him to go back to work. . . .

II

When Xuma got to the mines there was confusion everywhere. Myriads of lights glowed everywhere and a confusion of voices greeted him. Whistles blew and little groups of men moved about. He pushed his way through the men and saw that some of them belonged to Johannes' gang. Far ahead he saw the Red One. There must have been an accident.

He grabbed a man near him and shook him.

'What is it?'

'There is an accident,' the man said.

'Where is Johannes?'

'I don't know.'

'He's down there,' another man said.

Xuma pushed his way through till he stood beside Paddy.

Paddy grabbed his arm.

'Johannes and Chris are down there. I am going down.'

'I will go with you,' Xuma said.

'It is dangerous,' another white man said.

'Wait for the engineers to go,' the manager said.

'There are two men down there,' Paddy said and moved towards the little cage. Xuma followed him.

They got in and the cage shot down.

An ambulance arrived. Men stood by with stretchers. Two doctors waited. A hush fell over the crowd of waiting men. The mine manager kept looking at his watch. The minutes crawled by.

Five. . . . Ten. . . . Fifteen. . . . Twenty. . . .

Then they heard the cage coming up There was dead stillness as Xuma stepped out of the cage carrying the body of Johannes, and was followed by Paddy with the body of Chris

The doctors looked at Chris and Johannes. They were both dead.

'They kept the place up with their bodies so that we could get out!' a mine boy cried and began to sob.

Nobody paid any attention to him.

The two bodies were put into the ambulance. It moved off.

The tension in the air eased. Two engineers went down to inspect the damage. Silence hung over the crowds of waiting men. Again time crawled by. Paddy gave Xuma a cigarette.

The engineers came up.

'Well?' the manager asked.

'It was a minor collapse,' one of the engineers said. 'It's all right now. The beams were soaked through and rotten at one place. They gave. Nothing serious. If those fellows had kept their heads and stayed where they were instead of panicking and trying to keep the place open with their bodies, everything would have been all right. It is all right for working, anyhow, just a spot of clearing up and putting up new beams. The new shift can do that.'

The manager looked at the second engineer who nodded.

'They lost their lives through panic,' he said.

Paddy grabbed the man and felled him with one blow.

'They looked after their men,' he said. 'We warned you about that thing a long time ago.'

Men stepped between Paddy and the fallen engineer.

'All right! All right!' the manager cried. 'The mine's all right. Get ready to go down, night shift!'

'No!' Xuma cried. 'No!'

'Get ready!' the manager shouted.

'Let them fix up the place first!' Xuma cried. 'We warned them about it. They said it was all right. Now two men are dead! Good men! Let them fix it up first then we will go down!'

The manager looked at Xuma then at the rest of the mine boys. 'Get ready!' he shouted again.

'No!' a voice cried. 'Fix it up first!'

Xuma felt good suddenly. Strong and free. A man.

'We are men!' he shouted. 'It does not matter if our skins are black! We are not cattle to throw away our lives! We are men!'

'This is a strike!' the manager cried. He pointed at Xuma and shouted: 'You will go to jail! I have called the police! They will be here soon!'

'We will not go down if you say, so, Xuma!' a man shouted.

Xuma felt stronger than he had ever felt in all his life. Strong enough to be a man without colour. And now, suddenly, he knew that it could be so. Man could be without colour.

'Build up the place and we will go down!' he shouted. 'Build it up properly. Johannes was my friend! He was our friend! Now he is dead! Build up the place!'

'Those who are not striking come on this side!' the manager shouted and stepped to the left. All the indunas and the white men moved over to the left.

Only Paddy remained where he was. Xuma and the mine boys were on the right, the manager and the indunas and the other white men on the left. Paddy was in the centre.

'O'Shea!' the manager called.

It seemed that Paddy did not hear him.

'Come on, Paddy!' a white man called. 'It's all very well to play with them sometimes but we must show these kaffirs where they belong. Come on!'

This was what I argued with Di about, Paddy thought. This is the test of all my verbal beliefs. Zuma has taken the leadership, I must follow. Di was wrong about him. He's a man.

In the distance they could hear the siren of the police cars. Soon now the police would be there.

Paddy walked over to Xuma and took his hand.

'I am a man first, Zuma,' he said. Then he turned to the other mine boys and shouted: 'Zuma is right! They pay you a little! They don't care if you risk your lives! Why is it so? Is not the blood of a black man red like that of a white man? Does not a black man feel too? Does not a black man love life too? I am with you! Let them fix up the place first!'

Xuma smiled. Now he understood. He understood many things. One can be a person first. A man first and then a black man or a white man. . . .

Two pick-up vans swept into the mine yard and policemen swarmed out of them.

'There they are! Those two are the ring-leaders!' the manager shouted.

The indunas joined the policemen as they rushed on the crowd striking left and right with their batons.

Xuma saw a policeman strike Paddy across the back of the neck while another grabbed his arms and twisted them behind him. Then suddenly a policeman was close to him and he could not watch Paddy any more. Something stung his left shoulder and made his left arm limp with pain. He dodged a blow to his head and grabbed the policeman's arm. With a twist of his wrist he wrenched the baton from the policeman. The policeman went down. He felt a blow at the back of his head and trickle of warm blood running down his shirt.

His brain cleared suddenly. He should get away from here. He struck at a helmeted figure in front of him and moved on. Now he was on the outskirts of the fighting crowd. He could make a dash for it and be away. Then Paddy's voice drifted to him:

'Do not run away, Zuma!'

But feet were pounding behind him and the desire to be free was strong, so he ran. The pounding drew near so he ran faster. After a time no one followed him. Still he ran. His lungs felt as though they were bursting and his brain throbbed painfully. And he could still hear Paddy shouting:

'Do not run away, Zuma!'

Around him the streets were empty. He was alone in the world. He ran through empty street after empty street. Through Malay Camp, past Park Station. It was as though a devil was driving him. Tears of weariness burned in his eyes. Still he could not stop himself. Now he was near Maisy's place. He slackened his pace. When he got to Maisy's gate he walked, but very fast. He was in a hurry. He went through the little passage. There was very little time.

He knocked on her door. In a little while he saw a light, then

Maisy opened the door. When she saw his face all sleep vanished from her eyes.

'Xuma!'

'Hello, Maisy.'

She pulled him into the room and shut the door.

Ma Plank sat up in the corner of the room where she slept on the floor. Xuma noticed that she looked very much older.

Without a word Maisy got water and bathed his head. Ma Plank made tea on Maisy's little Primus stove. When he had drunk the tea Xuma told them what had happened.

'What are you going to do?' Maisy asked when he had finished.

'The Red One's in jail. I must go there too. It would be wrong if I do not go. I would not be a man then.'

'You are mad, Xuma,' Ma Plank said. 'Go to another city till it is all over. They will not get you.'

'No, Ma Plank. I must go. If I do not go I will not want to live for the disgust I will have against myself. I must go. The Red One is there. He is not a black man but he is going to jail for our people, how can I not go? And there are many things I want to say too. I want to tell them how I feel and how the black people feel.'

'They know how we feel. They will do nothing,' the old woman said.

'But they have not heard us say it. It is good that a black man should tell the white people how we feel. And also, a black man must tell the black people how they feel and what they want. These things I must do, then I will feel like a man. You understand?' He looked at Maisy.

She patted his hand and nodded.

'I understand, Xuma.'

He took her hand and looked into her eyes.

'You have always been good for me, Maisy. Now I know I love you and want you. Maybe you will wait for me and when I come back we will make a home, heh?'

'And Eliza?'

'She's a poor, unhappy one, that one, but it is finished. You are the one for me.'

Maisy smiled through her tears.

'I will wait for you, Xuma. If it is a long time or a short time I will wait for you. I will wait for you until you come back to me. Then we will make a home where there will be much laughter and much happiness Do not fear that I will see others. You are the one I want and I will wait for you every day and every night.'

'I will come back, for you are a good person to be with.'

Maisy slipped her arm through Xuma's and they sat like that for a while. Ma Plank poured herself another cup of tea and got into her blankets again. Then Xuma got up.

'Now I must go.'

'I will go with you as far as the police station,' Maisy said.

'No,' he said.

'Yes,' she said.

'Let her go,' Ma Plank said.

'All right.'

'And when you tell them, Xuma,' the old woman said, 'make it good, then Daddy will be proud of you.'

'Yes, tell them!' Maisy said. 'I will be there to listen.'

They went out and walked down the empty street. . . .

*

One by one the lights of Malay Camp were turned out. One by one the lights of Vrededorp and the other dark places of Johannesburg, of South Africa, were turned out.

The streets were empty. The leaning, tired houses were quiet. Only shadows moved everywhere. Only the quiet hum of the night hung over the city. Over Vrededorp. Over Malay Camp.